SEAGULLS HATE PARSNIPS

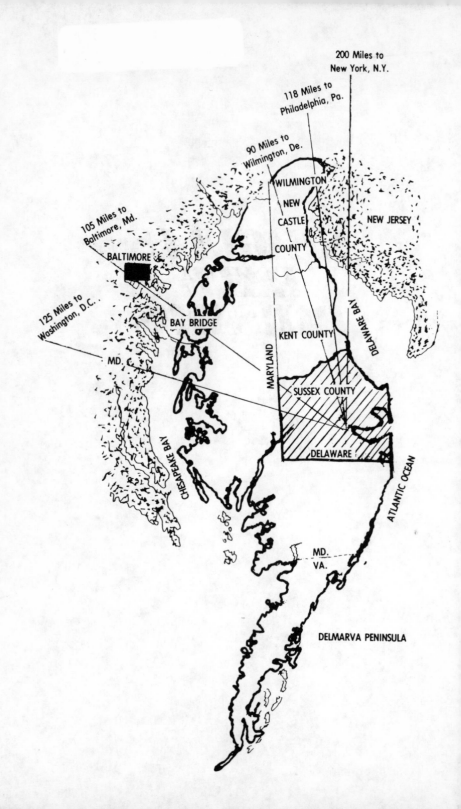

SEAGULLS HATE PARSNIPS

Offbeat and upbeat observations on life at the Delaware Shore.

by Virginia Tanzer

Illustrated By The Author

EPM
PUBLICATIONS, INC.

Other Books by Virginia Tanzer

Call It Delmarvalous
Capo Di Monte

Library of Congress Cataloging-in-Publication Data

Tanzer, Virginia.
  Seagulls hate parsnips.

1. Sussex County (Del.)—Description and travel.
2. Sussex County (Del.)—Social life and customs.
3. Atlantic Coast (Del.) 4. Gulls. I. Title.
F172.S8T3 1988   975.1'7   89-1214
ISBN-0-939009-23-4

EPM Publications, Inc., 1003 Turkey Run Road,
  McLean, VA 22101

Printed in the United States of America

CONTENTS

FIRST GLANCES

THE SEASONS

THE FEATHERS OVERHEAD

CODA

Author's Note to the 1989 Edition

In the eleven years since this book first appeared, there have been many changes. Frinstance:

Growth

The population of Sussex County has jumped from 80,000 to 110,000. What's more, estimates are that by the year 2010, Sussex County, with a projected population of 161,000, will be the second largest county in the state. It will thus out-people its neighbor to the north, Kent County, home of the state capital and the Dover Air Force Base.

Reflecting this population explosion, the 1988 telephone book for "Lower Delaware" had about 800 pages compared to the 510 pages in the 1983 edition. It is getting almost too big to hold comfortably.

Chicken processing, long a major industry in Sussex County, has also shown a flurry of feathered expansion. Two hundred million chickens are now raised annually in Sussex County. On the Delmarva Peninsula, 500 million chickens are grown each year, making the area the fourth largest chicken producer in the nation. (Arkansas, 1st; Georgia, 2nd; Alabama, 3rd.)

House Moving

The tendency of Sussex Countians to move houses around the countryside like shopping carts has in no way abated. In fact, a Lewes group has made a profession out of it, locating old houses around the state and moving them to Ship-carpenter Square in Lewes. This thriving area bristles with remodeled and modernized 18th and 19th century houses.

The Square is located right across from the Historical Complex in Lewes and is well worth a visit.

Indian Powwow

The Nanticoke Indian Powwow mentioned in Chapter 9 is now definitely established as an annual event of importance. Check the local calendars of events for the dates.

Traffic Trauma, Sussex Summer Snarl, Gasoline Gridlock
(Chapter 11)

The population explosion, of course, means that more and more of the county's farmlands and woods get Macadamized. Route One from Five Points South now looks like a developer's dream and/or an ecologist's nightmare. People can be heard giving directions to guests according to signs in the shopping centers. "Turn right," they'll say, "at the purple dinosaur" (an inelegant landmark in the "Sports Complex" bordering a road leading to a huge new housing development. And the heart breaks as shopping-mall-oriented bulldozers rip into yet one more old farmhouse, its big trees and clapboard outbuildings.

Away from the main routes, however, much rural beauty remains. In spite of the population pressures, Sussex County is still one of the treasured garden spots of the east coast. Not only that, in a world gone mad with "freedoms" and excesses, Sussex Countians cling to their standards of honor, virtue, and decency. Visiting there after time spent in any big city is like putting cool balm on sunburn. Long live the beauty of Saltwater Sussex!

I

FIRST GLANCES

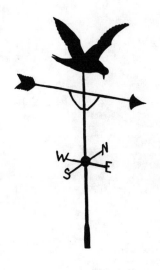

ONE

Sussex County, Where?

Most people in this country have never heard of Sussex County, Delaware. You might even say that swarms of people west of the Mississippi (and a lot east of it) have only the vaguest notion about what and where Delaware itself is. At the 1964 New York World's Fair, for instance, less than half the people questioned were able to identify Delaware as a state in the United States. They thought Delaware was the capital of Maryland, or something weird like that.

So, just to set this important matter straight, Delaware is a state. It is also the second smallest state in the nation. (Rhode Island captures first place.) But don't say pooh pooh just because the state is small and has only one Congressman. Big things come in small packages, and all that. Maybe the state is a geographical pin point, but it's a mighty sharp pin point. Quality, not quantity, is what counts. Just ask any Delawarean. (Maybe you'd better not put the question to a Texan or an Alaskan.)

Modern Americans may not appreciate fully all the state's wonders, but the fathers of our country did. Thomas Jefferson called Delaware "a jewel among the states". Another fore-

11

father, known as "The Milford Bard", expanded that statement to mean that Delaware is like a diamond. So Delaware is known as the Diamond State. And that ought to settle the matter. Diamonds are small but brilliant, aren't they?

But if you insist on having more modern proof of the state's unequalled charms, look at what the National Geographic said on a Bicentennial Map of the Mid-Atlantic states: "Nine miles across at its narrowest, and hardly a hundred miles long, Delaware can be traveled in a hurry. But don't try. Unexpected diversity in this second smallest of states offers too much merely to be speeded past. Delaware sparkles with multiple facets."

True, every word of it. And just as valid about Sussex County as about the whole state. But, for the moment, back to opinions by forefathers.

Jefferson also said that Delaware was "always disposed to counter revolution". By which he meant that the natives were feisty and had a mighty independence of spirit. This is as true today as it was then, and may account for the fact that Delaware was not satisfied with only one nickname. It is also called the Blue Hen State. It seems that during the American Revolution, the mascots for a renowned Delaware regiment were two fighting gamecocks. (That's the state bird, incidentally.) These gamecocks had been hatched from the eggs of a Delaware Blue Hen. To urge themselves into battle, the Delawareans tore into action shouting, "We're the sons of the Blue Hen, and we're game to the end." Which seems a little esoteric, but that's how it was. They never could be pushed into any mold, these Delawareans.

Anyway, Delaware is divided into three counties, each of which is quite different from the other two. Of these, Sussex County is the biggest, the southernmost, the most rural, and the feistiest. It is also the least spoiled by the doubtful advantages of twentieth century "progress". If map-painting is your hobby, you can still color Sussex County green rather than big-city-grey or suburb-blah.

You can color the county blue, too. For, in Sussex, there is water, water everywhere -- big water like the Delaware Bay and the Atlantic Ocean along the county's east coast; and miles and miles and acres and acres of smaller water all across the rest of the county. In Sussex there are at least seventy lakes and ponds, which is a lot of lakes and ponds, and over three dozen named rivers and streams, which is a lot of rivers and streams. And all the rivers and streams have who knows how many unnamed branches, which is a lot etc. Three small bays, in addition to the Delaware Bay, send long fingers of water far inland. There are also two man-made canals, and nobody has even attempted to count the number of coves, swamps, guts, marshes, landings, and ditches. The place is really water-logged. And most of the water can be surfed on, boated on, swum in, fished in, clammed in, picknicked at, and camped nearby.

And is. Which causes Sussex County, particularly eastern coastal Sussex, to undergo a population explosion every summer.

Off season, approximately 110,000 year-round human residents live in Sussex County's 950 square miles. (The exact

13

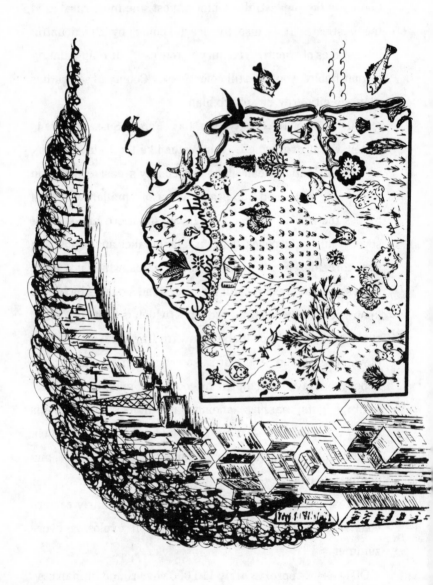

area varies depending on whether the tide is in or out.) This works out to be about seven or eight acres per person. Maybe Texans wouldn't call this the wide open spaces. Still, it means that Sussex Countians have enough elbow room to be feisty in. Which is important.

Three-quarters or more of the County's human inhabitants are rural. This means, obviously, that any population survey of the County should also include a healthy count of domestic animals, from horses and hogs to cows and chickens.

Particularly chickens. Sussex County broiler chickens outnumber humans about one thousand to one. The broiler industry, which wasn't even in existence here in 1920, today constitutes a major source of the County's income, and Sussex now raises from sixty to one hundred million chickens a year.

Rural rhythms and concerns dominate even the coastal residential areas. The whole County, not just its farmers, worries about drought, unseasonably heavy rain, or early frost. News programs end with quotations on light sows, heavy sows, and "Top Hawgs", or can begin with arresting statements such as "Mr. Farmer, Army worms are on the march!"

So, to this kind of background music, life during most of the year proceeds at a slow and dignified pace. But from Memorial Day through the summer, beach towns like Rehoboth suddenly find themselves bristling with an additional one hundred thousand or more open-space seekers. Year-round residents brace themselves for the onslaught. Shop and restaurant owners plan on long working hours, and hope for sizeable profits. Natives and the increasing number of retirees groan and complain about the long lines at check-out counters, restaurants, and movies. Traffic piles up into massive jams. On the hottest days, or on holidays, when beach-bound vehicles stretch bumper to bumper for miles, some bridge or other (see above on innumerable rivers and streams) invariably gets stuck in an "up" position. This causes both cars and their drivers to boil even more furiously.

Police, hospitals, and firemen stand on ever-ready alert. Every organization in need of money schedules what it earnestly hopes will be a successful program. (Read that to mean "fund-raiser".) And developers rub their hands in glee, dreaming of the time when they can bury the county under coats of macadam, and plaster the place with new architectural styles such as Factory Grey, Shopping Center Moderne, Trailer Park Primitive, Billboard Obscure, and High Rise Jungle.

By Labor Day, most of the brouhaha subsides. The county is weary and battered, but still green. Everybody gives a collective sigh and unwinds. The trampled dune grasses try growing again. Salt winds whoosh away the fumes and soot which have been spewing from thousands of car exhausts. And for three-quarters of a year, the county recovers from summer.

So far, the county's Atlantic coast line hasn't turned into a Miami Beach North, but there are many who wish it would. County politics are such that many people wonder if they are free of behind-the-scenes influence peddling. Developers want high-rises and other "pack-'em-all-in-close-together" features, and often seem to get the zoning variations they want in

16

spite of the howls and protests of nearby property owners.

Also lurking, ready to pounce on the still unspoiled shore line, are the Big Oil interests, their eyes aflame with visions of oil support facilities and other horrors. And to date, the attempts to control the predators in this inevitable growth have been of the hit-miss-and-hope-for-the-best variety.

At a recent meeting, sponsored by the Sussex County Council to promote oil support facilities along the coast, one oil company official was heard to remark, "These donkeys don't know what they're in for."

So the burning question is, will "these donkeys" start kicking, braying, and demanding intelligent and thoughtful planning for the future? If not, they will soon find themselves gobbled by the sprawling jaws of "progress". And one more pleasant way of life will have been dimmed by the high-rise shadow, and its green besmirched with the black spread of oil.

TWO

How Green Is My Sussex

Sussex County is a wonderful place. Other places are nice, too, but Sussex County is special.

Sussex is one of the few spots left in the world where everything isn't paved over, and where the moon doesn't rise over a skyscraper. Sussex County's windows open on corn fields and trees and birds and lakes and ocean. When grey skies hover over Sussex, you can be certain there are honest-to-goodness clouds up there about to spill moisture on the earth, not soot and gluck. When you breathe in Sussex, the stuff you inhale is still pretty much the way Mother Nature intended it to be.

Maryland's Eastern Shore is awfully nice, but not as nice as Sussex. Over there along the Chesapeake, brick Colonial mansions lift their rosy chimneys over almost every clump of trees. The famous and the rich spend millions adding modern bathrooms, swimming pools, and steel support-beams to neglected Eighteenth Century houses. People write rhapsodical volumes about the glories awash on Chesapeake Bay -- the skipjacks, the oyster tonging, the Blue Crabs, the sail boats, the log canoes. In between writing and remodeling, lots of good old Maryland hospitality abounds. Those who aren't invited to the aboundings settle for the annual house tours.

Sussex County isn't as glossy as the Eastern Shore. It has one thing they don't have, though -- the Atlantic Ocean. That temperamental watery charmer can hold down its side of the value scales any time.

New York City is nice, but not as nice as Sussex County. To get to the Big Apple, you have to scorch along sixteen-lane highways jammed disaster-close to other people's bumpers. If you obey the speed limit, barn-size trailer-tractors spew past you as if you weren't moving at all. All New York motorists suffer from snarling ulcers. They explode from lane to lane, venting their outrage that anyone else is on the road. You are so busy trying to avoid becoming a statistic, you always miss your turn-off, and the next exit is twenty miles ahead.

En route, you pass Elizabeth, N.J.

Acres of smut-stained smokestacks shouldn't happen to a town named Elizabeth.

New Jersey calls itself the Garden State, but it isn't as gardenny as Sussex County. No garden worth the tilling would have an Elizabeth in it. Even dandelions think twice before growing in the pavement cracks.

From Elizabeth, it's only a hop, skip, and a heart attack through megalopolis to the George Washington Bridge. Compared to the G. W. Bridge at rush hour, the tortures of Inferno seem like a description of Paradise.

There isn't a sign of megalopolis in Sussex County. The nearest thing to it lies along two-lane Route 26, where the highest structures to be seen are the town water towers, and where you have to go all the way through Bethany Beach, Ocean View, Millville, and Clarksville before you can spot a

19

good size corn field.

When you visit Manhattan, you find out that New Yorkers believe they are enjoying wonderful weather when they can dimly discern the outlines of the Empire State Building through the smog. Metropolitan gardeners spend a lot of time on their balconies washing soot off the potted plants. Only very courageous New Yorkers wear white gloves.

Manhattan is full of marvelous restaurants, theatres, and fascinating shops. You can get a nice lunch or buy a theatre ticket there for not much more than a week's salary.

People aren't very neighborly in New York. They can shop along Fifth Avenue all day without running into anybody they know. Sometimes, they are born, live and die without finding out who occupies the apartment next door. If a New Yorker gets sick and yells for help, his friendly neighbors close their windows so the screams won't interrupt the evening news.

When a Sussex Countian goes downtown, he runs into a lot of friends and gets caught up on the gossip. Secrets find their way awfully fast onto the Sussex County telegraph. The Sussex Countian has an ear quick to listen. He also has a heart slow to condemn. Being old-fashioned-virtue-oriented, the Sussex Countian knows that everybody lives in a glass house. People like each other in Sussex. Recovery from illness has a way of being delayed because of the steady stream of well-wishers dropping by with baskets of cup-custard.

New England is nice, but not as nice as Sussex County. To get to New England, you toll-booth northward.

Down East is full of picturesque rock-bound cliffs and delicious lobsters. Mornings in New England begin with breakfasts of baked beans, cod fish, and apple pie. But New Englanders never heard of scrapple. Those who have are scarcer than mountains on Delmarva. In all of New England, you can't buy a single, solitary package of scrapple. No Rapa scrapple. No Milton, Delaware, scrapple. No scrapple at all.

New Englanders are proud of being descended from the Puritans and have written a lot of history books telling how everything began on Plymouth Rock in 1620. Jamestown and the year 1607 mean nothing to New Englanders. And if you tell a Down Easterner about the 1631 settlement in Lewes, Sussex County, Delaware, he thinks you are making up the whole thing.

The deep South is nice, but not nearly as nice as Sussex County. Nobody in the world is more gracious and charming

than a real Southerner. Compared to Southerners, all the rest of us behave like bumbling clods, even when we are wearing our best, Sunday-go-to-meeting-company manners. People in the South don't have to worry much about winter clothes and high heat bills. But come spring, they spend days putting everything in plastic bags to keep the mildew out. Family trees are tightly twined around each Southerner's heart. You are considered a separate and unequal Yankee unless your grandfather fought for the Confederacy.

California and the West are nice, but not nearly as nice as Sussex County. If you tell a Californian you have been star gazing, he thinks you have taken a sight-seeing bus around Hollywood. Out West, they have hills and mountains all over the place. You keep reading in the papers about houses sliding down the hills into the sea. Everybody has faults, but they have the biggest one of all out in California. It's called San Andreas, and you never know when its going to go slipping and shaking things up a lot.

People in all those other places talk funny, too. In Brooklyn, you have to woik hard choosing between dese tings and dem tings. Faaathaa Narth, in Baaston, people pack their kazz in packing lots and send their smaatt children to baading skyules and then on to Have-id. In the deep sooth Suthinaz talk mosly the way Prezdin Cahtah and the Jahjans do. Out West, folks think "Yes" is pronounced "Yup" or "Yessirree", and are apt to aim a Colt 45 at you if you talk about "Frisco".

Sussex Countians have their own way of talking. If they have a little accent of their own, it has been passed on to them from their Old English ancestors. Also, they're proud of it. No

Sussex Countian wants to be pushed into any mold, let alone a speech mold. Sussex Countians believe in hard work, honor, and in themselves.

No matter whether they live to Millsboro or to O-Korchard, Sussex Countians think that if yur granpappy warn't barn in Delwur, you cain't be a real Delwurian. Sussex Countians have hoppers in thur bathrooms, zincs in thur kitchens, picters on thur walls, and wear gorgets round thur necks. Lots of people in the County are Volunteer Farmen, who shore do a good job fighting fars.

If thur fields gits fruz over, it's likely thur sweet pertaters and carn will git spurled. If you cain't find a Sussex Countian to home, you look this-a-way and that-a-way until somebody tells you he's to dinner up to Milford, but they'll have him to call you. Meanwhile, you kin make yurself to home and rest yur coat a while.

Wunst in a while, when a Sussex Countian gits a holt of some money, he may drive acrost the bridge to Balmur, Murlin. That's not too fur off, but, Oh! My Dear! he'd a like to nivver git thur. It's a wunner he dint git kilt. Jest arter the bridge, he had a blow-out and had to change the tar. It was colt, too, but that war the onliest thing to do, and he shore felt tarred before he got to home.

Home to Sussex County! Bounded on three sides by carn, chickens, and the Atlantic Ocean, and on 'tother side by staunch individualism which cain't be tore down.

The rest of the United States is tolerable enough, but you don't have to think twiced to know that ri cheer to Sussex County is the onliest place to live, anymore, or even to retar.

23

THREE

How To Live Happily Ever After In Sussex County

In order to be happy on moving to Sussex County, new residents quickly have to absorb a few fundamental facts. If they don't, they are in trouble, and will probably end up returning whence they came. So here are a few helpful suggestions for newcomers, week-enders, and any other foreigners who might be interested.

1. All over Delmarva, FLAT IS BEAUTIFUL! If you yearn for mountains and hills and things like that, try Colorado.

2. No matter how long you live here, or how involved you get in community life, you will never be considered a Sussex Countian. To qualify for that, your grandfather should have been born here. And even if he was, and your father was, but you, by some quirk of fate, were born in Pennsylvania, you will still be considered an outsider.

3. Watch what you say. An enormous percentage of Sussex County's 110,000 residents are kissing cousins. Almost every native of Sussex is related to a large proportion of other Sussex Countians. Family ties are close, even among thirty-eighth cousins twice removed. Consequently, you will find it a sobering experience to go running on and on about somebody only to find that the person you have been talking

TO is related to the person you have been thinking ABOUT. After that, you won't ever have much chance of being elected to the town council.

4. Courtesy is beautiful. Not only is is beautiful, it is also the generally practiced mode of conduct. Newcomers who try throwing their weight around in a big-city manner find that the Sussex County temperature changes quickly from warm welcome to cold shoulder.

5. If you yearn for constant exposure to a blaze of city lights and daily visits to large department stores, Sussex County is not for you. It does not follow, however, that Sussex should be considered a shopping desert. Almost everything you want can be found somewhere in the County. It merely isn't all concentrated in one crowded emporium. In Sussex, shops offering the most sophisticated merchandise have a way of being tucked in a corner of some soy bean field. You just have to learn where to look. This takes a little time, but it's fun learning.

6. Simplicity is beautiful. Flashing your bank roll around is OUT. Name-dropping is OUT. Bragging about past achievements is OUT. Thinking of Sussex Countians as country hicks is OUT. That Sussex Countian in shabby blue jeans riding a tractor across his corn field is in all likelihood as well educated and as widely traveled as you are. What's more, he could have, and often does have, assets in seven figures, an aeroplane for week-end jaunts, and living room walls covered with early Picasso drawings. That shop-owner in shirt sleeves could easily be a widely recognized archaeologist, numismatist, or artist. He may also call a number of the world's great

by their first names, and be able to trace his ancestry back to William the Conqueror. All that being the case, lofty condescension toward the natives is OUT.

7. Also OUT are complaints about the weather, or comparing a beautiful day to weather some place else. Nothing is more hackle-raising than a statement like, "Isn't it a gorgeous day! Just like California!" It's a Sussex County day, and Sussex County ought to get the credit for it.

Climate-wise, most of North America's climate runs to wild extremes, and few areas on this continent can produce weather much better than Sussex. California and Florida may have more sunny days, but Florida summers are next to unbearable, and California has earthquakes and terrible droughts. In the Middle West and New England, howling winters gobble up most of the year. Also, New Englanders believe in this myth about having cool summers. Reality is something else again. In Maine recently, for instance, the temperature reached one hundred and two in July! However, because of the "Cool Myth" most New Englanders wouldn't THINK of buying an air conditioner, let alone a fan, so the frequent humid, ninety-degree days you experience up there are a foretaste of INFERNO.

The winter of '77 excepted, heavy snowfalls and extended periods of cold are very rare in Sussex County. In summer, hot winds blowing from the west can bring some scorchers, but in Sussex, you are never far away from a cooling ocean, river or lake, So take a plunge, and stop complaining.

8. In Sussex, caring about your neighbor is beautiful. This includes not only ministering to him in sickness and trouble, at

26

which Sussex Countians excel. It also means being "au courant" about your neighbor's secrets, as well as on little events in his daily life. So if, on moving to Sussex, you think you are going to keep that skeleton locked in a closet, forget it. The closet door will be wide open within a week or two after your arrival. Or before. Not that the revelation will shock any Sussex Countian. He has seen most bones in a variety of closets many times before.

If anonymity is your desire, moving to Sussex will be a terrible mistake. Almost everybody knows almost everything else about everybody else. The County, or at least your section of the County, will know what you eat for breakfast, what parties you go to, how much you drink or don't drink, whether or not you have ever strayed from the straight and narrow path, and if so, with whom. They will also know a great deal about a vast number of inconsequential details of your daily life. You can hardly change your brand of toothpaste in Sussex without the word's getting around and occasioning a number of comments about the wisdom or lack of wisdom of your decision to change.

Take "L'Affaire Commode", for instance. Recently, we decided it would be convenient to have some kind of inexpensive "facilities" in a studio room which is not connected to the main house. This seemingly quite personal decision occasioned a veritable Vesuvius of advice. As they say in literary circles, the names in the following little story have been changed to protect the innocent, but the facts are facts.

Barely had we mentioned to a friend our unglamorous hankering after a chamber pot than the phone began to ring.

First, we got three separate calls telling of people who might have old chamber pots in their attics they would loan us. Next came a call saying we were making a mistake to get a chamber pot. What we needed was a commode. Another person then called to say that he'd heard we were looking for commodes, and that Montgomery Ward had a splendid selection of commodes -- best, better, and good. In addition to which, this caller said, he had checked with Elias Johnson, the manager there -- we remembered Elias Johnson, didn't we? His wife, Mildred, was Post Mistress at Milton for a while, and her maternal grandmother was related in a direct line to Pocahontas, which made Mildred a thirty-second part Indian. Anyway, if we'd call Elias at Monkey Ward by 11 A.M. that day, we could pick up the new appliance day after tomorrow.

As we were lifting the receiver to do just this, the phone rang again. On the other end of the line was a well-wisher with the news that the Smiths used to have a very professional-type commode which they had bought for their mother-in-law when she was sick. Would we want to borrow it?

Alas, this generous idea came to naught. Several calls later, we learned that the Smiths had given their mother-in-law's commode to some cousins in Western Sussex, and they wished they hadn't because the cousins hadn't taken good care of it. The mother-in-law was now in a nursing home in northern Delaware, some place where they wouldn't let you smoke. As the Smith's mother-in-law had smoked like a furnace all her life (it was probably what made her give out so early, our caller said. She's only eighty now, and most of her family lived well into their nineties.) And because the mother-in-law couldn't smoke, she hated every pink inch of it up there in Northern Delaware.

Feeling both regret and relief, and definitely entangled in the mother-in-law's problems, we hurriedly placed an order for the "good" commode.

"L'Affaire Commode" happened several months ago, but we still keep running into people in grocery stores who inquire about it. Our latest grocery news flash concerned a commode which was fashioned of elaborately carved oak and belonged to a Mr. Engelbrock's great grandfather. When the Engle-brocks moved to Sussex, they had the work of art sterilized, and now use it as an ice bucket, with great social success.

So don't forget, in Sussex County, your life is an open book and Sussex Countians are good readers.

However, if newcomers will just remember the few fundamental hints given above, they will find Sussex County a marvelous place to live. If you want to buy a chamber pot, though, don't breathe a word about it in advance.

FOUR

The Temperamental Sorceress

Sussex Countians, particularly eastern Sussex Countians, dote on ocean watching. At any time of the year, come rain, come snow, come wind, come calmth, many of them can be found at vantage points along the coast taking a little check on what kind of a show the Atlantic is putting on that day. And when something really dramatic occurs, such as the infrequent, wondrous spectacle of the ocean's being covered with ice as far as you can see, ocean watchers turn out in vast numbers to look, to marvel, and to appreciate. The Atlantic is like a fascinating and dangerous woman. She keeps everybody guessing, and you can never tell what she is going to do next.

Back in November, 1968, the Atlantic put on quite a performance when a memorable Nor'easter raised a lot of commotion along the coast. Winds were clocked in gusts of up to 100 m.p.h., which, whatever you say, constitutes a breeze worth respecting. The howling roar was ear-splitting. Water in toilets sloshed wildly. Windows groaned and rattled. Loosened boards and shingles flapped and banged and blew away. If you stuck your head out the door, you discovered it was next to impossible to remain upright against the wind. Huge

31

branches, sections of roofs, and various other potentially deadly weapons were flying all over the place, so to venture outside was indeed to flirt with peril.

Radio announcers kept telling people to stay inside. But then those same announcers made a grave mistake. They didn't know their Sussex Countians. Obviously unaware of the numbers of people smitten with ocean-watching fever, the announcers broke into regular programs to report that a two-hundred-foot Norwegian oil barge with two stranded crewmen aboard had blown ashore at the foot of Virginia Avenue in Rehoboth Beach.

An oil barge beached right in the middle of town! What respectable ocean watcher could resist that? Before you could say "anemometer", hundreds of people had bent into the wind, fighting their way to the scene of action, and gathering along the shuddering and shredding boardwalk. Twenty-to-thirty-foot waves pounded over the barge and thundered against the boardwalk. You could feel the boards beneath your feet shaking and protesting.

At this point, one of the watchers, Father Richard Bailey, of All Saints' Episcopal Church, managed to shout over the deafening gale one of the dry comments for which he is famous, (thus furnishing the only dry thing around) "The only thing wrong with storm watching is that the weather is always so awful!"

But who could leave? Drenched with rain and salt water, buffeted by the wind, and apprehensive that at any moment the boards underfoot might be swept into the watery fury, everybody stood his highly unstable ground to watch the

drama unfold. Two Norwegian crewmen were still aboard
that barge. Were they to perish in that raging sea, or could
they somehow get ashore?

Suddenly, all the several hundred people along shore began
to yell and point. One of the Norwegians, trying to race from
below deck to a small structure topside, had been washed
overboard into the slamming breakers. Onlookers' hearts
stopped. A goner! But, No! Bursting through the watchers, a
man plunged into the ocean violence.

The intrepid rescuer was a mild mannered Rehoboth Beach
volunteer fireman whom no one had hitherto suspected of
heroic qualities. Somehow, this valiant was able to reach the
crewman, but discovered him so thickly coated with oil it was
next to impossible to hang onto the now unconscious man.

1

2

Photography by Howard Ennis

3

4   *Photography by Howard Ennis*

Gasping and struggling, the fireman got the Norwegian to within thirty feet of land, where other volunteers were able to drag them both ashore. Everybody along the boardwalk cheered, clapping his hands and pounding his neighbor on the back. An ambulance was standing by, and the seaman was whisked away to the nearby Beebe Hospital in Lewes, where he eventually recovered.

The collective feeling of relief didn't last long, however. What of the man still left on board, huddling inside the little topside cabin? How could he remain conscious while being banged violently from wall to wall? Each time one of the mountainous waves crashed over the barge, all eyes strained through the ensuing clouds of mist to see if the cabin had survived or had been splintered and washed away.

Soon, the boardwalk telegraph had it that a Coast Guard rescue heliocopter was on its way. But how would the pilot know the crewman was in the cabin? The barge was two hundred feet long, and the topside structure was only a few feet square. And how could the Norwegian fight his way through the tons of water pounding onto the barge to climb into a flimsy rescue basket?

Nobody would leave with these momentous questions unanswered. For several hours, everybody stood around wetly, discussing various methods of rescue, and scanning the turbulent horizon for the heliocopter. At last it hove into view. Loud cheers from the crowd. Each person on that boardwalk felt personally responsible for the success of the rescue. The tension was visible in the taut stances and straining positions of all the watchers.

Fighting the wind, the 'copter went to the wrong end of the barge. Suspense among the onlookers increased. Everybody jumped up and down, pointing to the cabin and shouting, "No! No! Not down there! Over here! In the cabin!"

It seems doubtful that the pilot gained any insight from the horde of Boardwalk Superintendents. But then again, perhaps the very force of all that united thought went straight to the pilot's brain, for shortly he changed direction, bringing the 'copter directly over the cabin.

"Watch out! Watch out!! everybody yelled. "Try to pick him up between waves! Easy! EEEEasy! If one of those breakers hits him, he's gone!"

Slowly, the basket lowered, swinging wildly in the wind. Somehow, and quite miraculously, the Norwegian battled his way from the cabin to the dangling rope. The minute the crewman swung himself into the basket, the pilot raised it, clearing by a split second a monstrous wave which thundered over the barge. Wild hurrahs and cheers from the boardwalk. Victory achieved!

Shortly, everyone seemed to feel cold and exhausted from his hours of rescue effort. People began to drift away, seeking hot coffee, warmth, and home. Before long, the boardwalk and the barge were left alone with the shrieking wind and the raging surf.

Viewing the Atlantic is not always so spectacular. But with or without stranded barges and imperiled lives, there's nothing like it, ocean watching. Beats television every time.

FIVE

Rehoboth Beach ....
Its First Two Thousand Years

Delaware's Rehoboth Beach has been attracting summer visitors for at least twenty centuries. It is easy to see why, for, along the mid-Atlantic coast, Rehoboth sits on one of the few areas where the mainland reaches the ocean. This geographical good fortune means that tree-bearing soil rolls right up to the dunes, giving nourishment to Rehoboth's marvelous pines, hollies, and red cedars. A wide variety of deciduous trees has also learned how to survive the salt winds. As a result, Rehoboth ends up with a combination hard to beat -- ocean, sandy beaches, and trees.

Age tests run on archaeological finds have shown that at least as early as the beginning of the Christian era, Indians found the area to be an attractive spot for summer pow-wows. The Nanticoke tribes of the Algonquin nation were regular warm weather visitors, escaping from the hotter inland temperatures, and enjoying a lot of fishing, clamming, and feasting. Evidence of all this is to be found in the burial grounds and the numerous middens of clams and oyster shells which lie scattered along the coast line.

The Nanticokes might also have had a permanent winter

colony. Long stone ice axes have been discovered near Rehoboth's lakes, which would indicate some sort of winter activity such as fishing. And, like modern year-rounders, the Indians probably looked forward every October to the arrival of the Canada Geese and the migrating ducks. For among its assets, Rehoboth can count that of lying directly on the path of the Atlantic Flyway. Nowadays, hundreds of ducks and geese winter on Rehoboth's two lovely little bodies of fresh water -- Lake Gerar and Silver Lake. The wildfowl rest on the lakes during the day, and at night feed on corn from the surrounding fields. Inasmuch as the Indians grew corn while Europeans still thought that anything pronounced "kernel" had to do with a military rank, it seems likely that wintering ducks and geese must have gladdened the spirits and added to the feasts of the Nanticokes as well as to those of Twentieth Century inhabitants.

No Indian name for the Rehoboth area seems to have survived. But in the mid-1600's, new settlers arriving from Europe named the bay just south of the present city limits "Rehoboth", which is a biblical word meaning "room enough". (Judging from later events, this apparently meant room enough for European settlers, but not by any means enough for the native Indians.) On its formation in the nineteenth century, the town of Rehoboth took its name from the bay.

It has long been considered historical fact that the first colonists of the area were Dutch, who in 1631 established a fort in Lewes, a few miles away from Rehoboth. These brave souls didn't last too long, alas. In their first winter, they got into a

dispute with the Indians over the insignia of the Dutch crown, with the unfortunate result that the settlers were all massacred.

However, it has recently been established that Europeans settled in eastern Sussex County long before the 1631 colony. Dr. John Witthoff, Curator of Eastern U.S. Indians Studies at the University of Pennsylvania Museum, has done extensive work in the area, and has unearthed evidence showing that as early as 1550, sailors jumped ship from vessels lying off shore, and took up residence on land.

It was, therefore, from these swashbuckling, tough, and illiterate tars that the East Coast Indians gained their first impressions of Europeans, and had a tendency to judge all other colonists accordingly. From this data, it is possible to surmise that the massacre of the 1631 settlers in Lewes was, at least partially, triggered by the Indians' distrust and dislike of the sea-going rapscallions who had preceded them.

In any event, shortly after their arrival, our American forebearers, whether of colonist or sea-faring ilk, soon began to act as if the land belonged to them and not to the natives. So by the end of the seventeenth century, most of the poor Indians had been pushed out as the new settlers took over the land for farming.

Come to think of it, things haven't changed much in three hundred years. The reason for being here may have changed from colonization to vacationing, but when twentieth century summer visitors swarm into Rehoboth, they also have a tendency to act as if the place existed just for their particular pleasure. Somebody ought to do a study on the Dr. Jekyll and

Mr. Hyde transformation which seems to take place in humans going on holiday trips. People who are apparently God-fearing, law-abiding pillars of their communities back home seem to turn into fiends the minute they hit a summer resort. They strew garbage, cans, and broken bottles on driveways, break up lawn furniture, use residents' front yards as bathrooms, and steal anything lying around loose.

Why is that?

Where were we? Ah, yes, back on the Rehoboth farmland. The new settlers bent their backs to the plows. Any idea of developing a summer resort took a back seat to wresting a living from the land, and to engaging in a series of wars -- the first for independence, the second also against the English, and the third between the states. (Historical note: In 1813, nearby Lewes was bombarded for twenty-two hours by the British Fleet. Fortunately for Lewes, the British gunnery officer needed new glasses or something, for the results were "one chicken killed, and one pig wounded, leg broken".)

After all these military operations got themselves straightened out, however, the way was cleared for concentration on Rehoboth's development as a summer resort. Several early attempts to lay out a town seem not to have gotten much further than a gleam in a few Nineteenth Century developers' eyes. But in 1872, the Methodists decided Rehoboth would make a wonderful location for a Camp Meeting site. As it is next to impossible to swerve a determined Methodist from his inspired path, development proceeded apace. An association was formed. Money was raised. Four hundred acres of land were purchased for a little under $10,000, (which today would

42

hardly pay for enough Rehoboth land on which to put a pulpit) and in 1873, the Delaware Legislature recognized the new "Rehoboth Beach Camp Meeting Association".

Soon, hundreds of lots had been sold and frames for tents had been built in an area near the Canal. Several years later, a tabernacle seating five hundred people was built in the center of town. Some narrow, two-story summer houses were nailed together near the tabernacle. A few of these still stand much as they were over a hundred years ago. One such Camp Meeting house has been moved to Christian Street, where it presently serves as the Rehoboth Museum.

Human nature being what it is, people back in 1875 soon found ways to make the Methodists' "Thou Shalt Nots" into "Thou Shalts". Hotels which recognized the profits to be reaped from temptations of the flesh and bottle sprang up a few feet outside the Methodist limits. Houses other than the Camp Meeting type began to appear. The numbers of both summer visitors and year-round residents have continued to grow ever since, at first gradually, but lately at an ever-increasing speed.

Summer Sundays in today's Rehoboth, with everything except booze stores going full tilt, make it difficult to realize that Rehoboth began with by-laws which read, "The Sabbath shall be sacredly observed, and no traffic or recreation in violation thereof shall be lawful". It is true that, over the years, Camp Meeting Methodists have been out-numbered by people with a more comfortable relationship with sin, but it is probable that, because of the original Methodist influence, Rehoboth has remained, by and large, a family town, and has not been taken over completely by the purveyors of razz-a-ma-tazz.

In the late 1800's, expansion of the resort came slowly. Mosquitos may have deterred some potential buyers. These unwelcome inhabitants had things pretty much their own way until serious mosquito control work was undertaken in the Nineteen Thirties. Mosquitos are strong on survival, however, and even today the city fathers find it necessary to spray the town before big holidays. (By the way, have you ever reflected on the fact that many bugs, like the mosquito, which are way down near the bottom of the ecological food chain themselves, survive by dining off animals at the top of the food chain like humans and other mammals? Which musing ought to insert a little humility into your top-of-the-food-chain ego.)

Another factor to put a lid on bubbling development was the circumstance that, until after World War I, the area was hard to reach. Before the building of the north-south Coleman duPont Boulevard through the state around 1920, people mainly arrived in Rehoboth by railroad. Meeting the train and picking up the mail furnished a high point on a summer's day. At the train stop, you could see all your neighbors, hear the latest gossip, and plan future parties and excursions. Off-season in today's Rehoboth has much the same folksy flavor. The focus of a train's arrival may be missing, but on any jaunt into town you are bound to see a lot of people you know and to pick up the latest hot news items. A good deal of politicking and planning takes place on street corners or in front of the Post Office, and, hopefully, always will.

In 1925, accessibility to Rehoboth was increased when a

paved road was brought in from the west. Steamboats from Baltimore to the Delmarva Peninsula were supplanted first by the Chesapeake Bay Ferry, and then by the Bay Bridge. Prices of land and the number of both summer visitors and year-round residents have increased in direct ratio to the area's accessibility. Air service has been introduced. Highways continue to be widened and improved. More and more tourist accommodations have been built, until nowadays Rehoboth jumps to a population of around 125,000 in the summer, making it the second largest city in the state during the warm weather months.

The increase in population, of course, has brought with it some of the problems which beset metropolitan areas. However, it can be argued that this loss of a gentler, slower way of life is offset by the more sophisticated advantages it produces. In 1938, the Delaware Guide listed Rehoboth as having "Year round activities . . . (of) a laundry, a clothes cleaning plant, two dairies, a bank, and a large cannery" -- hardly a shopper's paradise! Today in Rehoboth, many attractive shops, restaurants, hotels, and theatres stay open year-round, and the Post Office delivers winter mail to around fifteen thousand people.

Leaving out the summer vacationers, for the moment, it can certainly be said that people who are attracted to a life by the ocean have inherent in them independence of spirit, and a desire for a more relaxed life-style than is possible in more urban surroundings. Both old-time residents and new transplants have deep loyalty to and great interest in their community. They feel personally involved in the way

45

Rehoboth grows. Whatever the issue -- zoning, beach fees, sewers, schools, conservation, off-shore oil drilling -- everybody turns out to debate it. At one hearing about off-shore drilling, crowds jammed Rehoboth's Convention Hall to overflowing. One visitor was heard to say, "Good night! Look at this mob! People here give a damn, don't they?"

And indeed they do. Rehoboth, even at the height of the summer influx, still has charm -- a town of pleasant houses and gardens, of mostly gentle people with a broad scope of interests and activities; a place with the charisma which comes from that magical combination of trees, sand, and ocean waves.

SIX

A Wilmingtonian's Idea
Of Sussex County

One burning question in this southern part of the state probably flames just as fiercely in rural areas all over the country. Around here, the steaming bone of contention is: Do Northern Delawareans think Sussex County is a part of Delaware, or don't they? From all you hear, northern state residents think of Sussex as a kind of wild and untamed hinterland with the cultural advantages of, say, Patagonia or deepest Mongolia. Apparently "up there" they think civilization stops just below Wilmington at the Chesapeake and Delaware Canal. Maybe they should update Caesar to read "Delawaria in partes duas divisa est". And by the two parts, they mean "Upper" and "Lower".

That's a downright snobbish way of distinguishing between two areas of a state, isn't it? It's like talking about the upper and lower crust. Who wants to be referred to as a "lower Delawarean"? Does that put everybody in Sussex County in the same class with the lower animals, the lower vertebrates, the lower orders? Or what?

There you have it. And it is obviously the prevailing attitude upstate. When the "Today" show presented its Bicentennial series on the fifty states, for instance, everything that matters

47

was portrayed as taking place entirely in upper Delaware. "Lower" Delaware, referred to as "BELOW THE CANAL", was made out to be a kind of swampy boondocks with a little bit of ocean alongside.

A sad angle is that Southern Delawareans have been brainwashed into accepting this "upper" and "lower" stuff. Radio announcers, for instance, usually say that weather in "lower Delaware" will be such and such. Why not "Southern" instead? Or even "Downstate"? "Rain expected Downstate" is a lot less condescending than all those references to lower Delaware.

Guidebooks printed about Delaware also always seem to use the haughty lorgnette approach to Sussex County. Take books like "Fun In The First State" or the "Go, Don't Go Guide to Delaware and Nearby Pennsylvania". From the titles, you would assume, wouldn't you, that the authors intended to cover the whole state of Delaware? Not so. Authors of Delaware guidebooks constantly use the "upper" and "lower" syndrome. Hundreds of places are listed for northern Delaware. When they get to Sussex County, the numbers of things to see dwindle to the reluctant naming of a tiny number of jolly spots, mostly State Forests and Wildlife areas. Sussex certainly has these, thank goodness. But it can also hold its own on matters of "cultchah".

When they talk about "Art", for instance, these handbooks of information have never heard of the Rehoboth Art League; the Woodbridge Art League; the Sussex County Arts Council; the innumerable classes in music, dance, and the arts, offered in places like the Rehoboth Art League or the Community

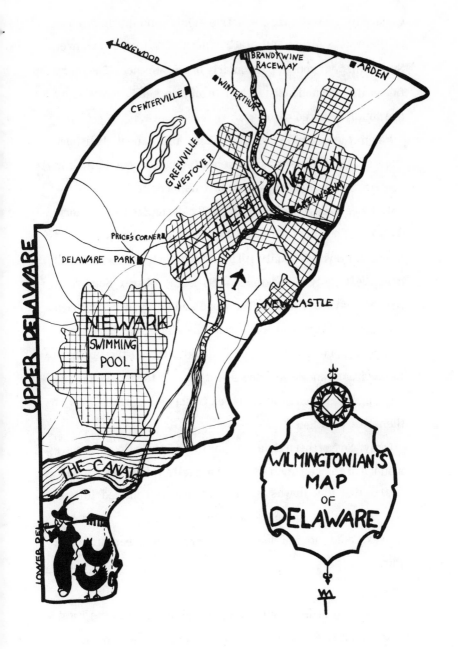

UPPER DELAWARE

LONGWOOD

BRANDYWINE RACEWAY

ARDEN

WINTERTHUR

CENTERVILLE

GREENVILLE
WESTOVER

WILMINGTON

MUSEUM

PRICE'S CORNER

DELAWARE PARK

NEWARK
SWIMMING
POOL

NEW CASTLE

THE CANAL

LOWER DEL.

WILMINGTONIAN'S
MAP
OF
DELAWARE

49

College in Georgetown; the active theatre and music groups; or the dozens of art and crafts shows which burst out over Sussex all year round, particularly in the summer. The many fine craftsmen and artists who live and work in Sussex County are totally ignored also.

When these Delaware Baedekers talk about "Historic Places", there usually isn't even a footnote about Bethel, in eastern Sussex County, which just happens to be one of the only three Delaware towns officially designated as Historic Areas. (The other two are New Castle in the north, and Lewes, in Sussex County.) The active Historic Societies all over the County are skipped. So is the Sussex Society of Archaeology and History. The Woodland Ferry, which carried the famous Patty Cannon across the Nanticoke River, and which still runs, might be in Timbuktu, for all the northern Delawareans know. And how about some of the marvelous old buildings scattered around Sussex County? Forget it. Few of them are mentioned.

Okay. So Northern Delawareans think Sussex Countians are a bunch of chicken farmers who can't tell a Renoir from a barn board, and that downstate architecture is confined to wigwams and silos. At least, you would imagine, they would give Sussex County its full due when it comes to "Recreation and Parks."

Ha!

It's hard to believe, but if the readers of "Fun in the First State" want to go swimming, this guide says they should try the University of Delaware's outdoor pool in Newark. Or, they say, try an apartment house complex, many of which have pools. That's all for swimming. Period. Apparently Sussex County's built-in outdoor pool eighteen miles long and two thousand miles wide doesn't count. Not to mention all the rivers, streams, lakes, and other natural swimming holes spread around the County.

And if you want to play golf or tennis, if you want to ride horseback, bicycle, canoe, bowl, hike, fish, or boat, you'd better play it safe and stay north of the Canal. None of these activities is mentioned as occurring in Sussex. Northern Delawareans must think we spend all our recreation time in jousting at tournaments or in other medieval pastimes.

Oh, well. The only thing you can say, I guess, is that the poor dears don't know what they're missing. Maybe it's just as well. If they ever found out what Sussex County has to offer, they would be rushing down here every pink moment, and end up ruining the place.

SEVEN

Don't Like Where Your House Is?
Move It.
It's Done Every Day In Sussex.

Here is a nice brain twister. One summer, an oil company decides it needs to move a twenty-thousand gallon steel storage tank to a new location. It is a huge thing, with a diameter of approximately fifty feet, and a height of about forty to fifty feet. To make the trip, the tank will be jacked onto supporting timbers. When it reaches its new site, the tank must rest solidly on the ground, with no air pockets underneath it. If there are holes underneath it, the bottom of the tank will rust and its structure be severely weakened.

Now here's the facer. How do you get the tank off the supporting timbers onto level ground without leaving large grooves in the earth as you pull the timbers out from under the tank?

While you are trying to figure out the answer, it might interest you to know that engineers with the Sun Oil Company, to whom the tank belonged, said it absolutely could not be done. Better build a new tank, they said. There was a way, though. Any ideas on how it was done? No?

Well, a remarkable Sussex Countian came up with an answer, and it worked. He was Charles E. Marvil, of Laurel, Delaware, who moved houses, boats, oil tanks, or whatever, up into the air, over water, and across the Delmarva Peninsula as if they were toy scenery surrounding a Lionel train set.

Here is how Charles Marvil solved that storage tank problem. He moved it, still on its timber supports, directly over the new location. He smoothed the ground under it carefully. He hauled in a vast quantity of ice in three-hundred pound blocks, placing them under the tank. He then braced the tank, so it wouldn't slide off, and lowered it directly on the ice. That done, he went home to bed. Next morning when he returned, summer heat had done its work, and there sat the tank, firm and snug in its place.

Two of Charles Marvil's sons, C. Robert and Norwood Marvil, have continued in their father's house moving paths, with the result that Sussex County has to be one of the house-movingest places in the world. Many are the tales of prodigious feats, such as hauling a seventy-five foot yacht from the ocean where it had run aground, across shifting dunes to Chincoteague Bay; (The Coast Guard had given up on this one.) or hoisting a ninety-ton oil burner twenty-two feet into the air for the electric company; or squeaking a wide house across the Dewey Beach bridge with only four inches to spare.

It is almost impossible to stand on any corner of Rehoboth Beach or Lewes, or almost any Sussex County town, with either Bob or Norwood Marvil without their saying, "You see that house over there? Well it used to be down on Surf Avenue." (Or, "down the road a mile"), or "We moved it here from Georgetown (or Bridgeville, or Ocean City, or out in the country").

53

And you can't be long in Sussex without meeting up with one of the Marvil's houses rolling ponderously down the highway, looking for all the world like some Juggernaut out of an old Cecil B. deMille extravaganza. (Your imagination can supply the chanting throngs, assorted Christian martyrs inextricably attached to something in the direct path of the oncoming monster, to be saved in the nick of time by our hero in toga, tunic, or flowing robe.)

Figures vary, but the Marvils move around fifty houses a year, and they are not the only ones so engaged. A firm in Angola moves houses. So does another in Millsboro. Frequently, private individuals buy old garages or barns, rig up some wheels, and set forth across flat Sussex County to give the building new life in another location. So as you can see, house moving is as Sussex Countian as chickens, the ocean, and apple pie.

Three things seem to account for this constant shuttling of buildings all over the place -- flat land, lots of frame houses (which are easier to move than brick structures) and, of course, the fact that there are available in Sussex County house movers like the Marvils who make it all seem like a piece of cake.

Charles Marvil once had a customer who worried about what might happen to his dishes and other breakables if he were to leave them in the house while it was being moved. In answer to this, Charles put a glass of water on a table in the house, telling the customer that if the water spilled during the move, there would be no charge. Needless to say, the water remained in the glass and the customer paid up.

Some people insist on staying in their houses during the move. One woman even baked a cake while she and her house were in motion. The cake didn't fall and was very tasty, Bob Marvil reports. A seventy-six-year-old man had a house sixty by sixty feet, three stories high. It was full of pictures and priceless antiques. The gentleman wanted to move the building only a short distance away, but was afraid of theft if he were to move out of it.

He arranged, therefore, with the electric company to put service on a long wire. He and his wife (no spring chicken either) climbed into the house on ladders during the months it took to get the house ready for moving. (The house was so large and heavy it required ten steel beams and forty wheels under it.) On moving day, the elderly gentleman and his wife sailed off across the fields without one of his whiskers being ruffled, or one of his cups cracked.

All house movers are not so successful. In Rehoboth Beach today, a house which sits on a little hillock at the corner of Olive Avenue and First Street, used to face the ocean on Surf Avenue (now the Boardwalk). After the 1918 storm, which was a doozey like the 1962 storm, the foundation of the house was undermined. The owner decided to move it inland.

The house got as far as half a block up Virginia Avenue, when the mover, for unstated reasons, decided the whole thing was too much. So he quit. The house sat in the middle of Virginia Avenue all summer long, undoubtedly furnishing a lively conversation piece for vacationers. Finally, someone had the inspiration to call Charles Marvil, who whisked it around the corner and jacked it up to its present location.

The Marvils' success in moving large structures has rested not only on their ingenuity, but also on their knowledge and their extreme care with every detail. One of their secrets has been that they use a "three point load" -- two wheel units in the rear, and one wheel unit in the front. When a four-point load is used, there is danger of wrenching the house, if, for instance, one of the front wheel units were to go in a rut.

The front wheel unit used by the Marvils is a miracle of engineering in itself. It consists of eight large wheels with rubber tires to cushion the ride (the Marvils added the tires) These eight wheels are held together by a steel axle which can make a three-hundred-sixty-degree turn, thus giving a size-able house a turning circle hardly larger than that of a big automobile.

Up until 1930, horses were used to move houses. The method then was to attach the house by block and tackle to a large windlass, called a "crab". The crab was held firm by large iron spikes being driven through it into the ground. A horse was placed on a "sweep", and walked around and around the crab (taking care to step over the cable) until the house was cranked up to the windlass location. The crab was then moved forward. The spikes were again driven into the ground, and the whole operation was repeated and repeated until the house got where it was trying to go. In those times, the wheels under the house were heavy wooden rollers made out of holly.

In addition to wheel improvement, modern invention has introduced a motorized winch attached to the back of a heavy truck. This winch can be used when a lot of manoeuvering must be done to get a house to a pin-point location over its

Photography by Chuck Snyder

Photography by Chuck Snyder

Photography by Chuck Snyder

foundation or basement.

Here, a momentary digression, as it is impossible for me to type the word "winch" without recalling a college freshman I knew in years past. This aspiring author was assigned the task of writing a paper on his activities over the summer. He had, it developed, taken a freighter trip through the Panama Canal. His ship must have loaded and unloaded a lot of cargo, for the student wrote that night after night he was kept awake by the "squealing and groaning of the wenches".

But back to house moving. It is true that recent inventions have added manoeuverability and greater ease to house moving. It is also certain, however, that technological advancement has complicated the business of transferring a large object from one place to another by stringing utility wires and traffic lights across roads and intersections. Even a short move from location "a" to spot "b" is fraught with innumerable hazzards.

Several years ago, for instance, the Marvils moved a Rehoboth Camp Meeting house only two blocks through the center of town, ending at a new location on Christian Street where the building now serves as the Rehoboth Beach Museum. In this trek, such problems as getting locked, parked cars off the street were pesky but minor. The police hauled the cars away. But the rest of the obstacles made for a house moving that, to the uninitiated at least, was more exciting than a suspense movie.

Just getting the house off its lot and onto the street was tense-making. The ground was muddy and soft, so a path of planks had to be kept in front of all the sixteen wheels under the house. To do this, men swarmed under the MOVING house, arranging and re-arranging heavy boards so the wheels could roll ahead smoothly. Sometimes, the men were only inches ahead of the oncoming wheels. A split second later, the huge, heavy wheels would crunch over the spot where the men's heads or hands had been.

But obstructions overhead proved to be the real heart-stoppers. Anyone watching Bob or Norwood Marvil during the many moments of crisis would not be aware of the drama involved. Both men appeared calm as a windless summer day. Their pulse rates may have gone up alarmingly, but the only outward indication of their tension was that, with the temperatures around thirty-four chilling degrees, both men took off their coats and mopped their brows after the house was safely across Rehoboth's main intersection.

As the house rolled along, Bob Marvil constantly moved so that he could be seen at all times by the truck driver, who at that time was a wonderfully skilled man named Homer Duncan. Bob directed the driver by hand signals, very much like a flight officer waving a plane into a landing. Sometimes, there were also word instructions. "Hold it! HOLD IT!" "Back 'er up, Homer" "Go ahead an inch, Homer!" (Incidentally, could you drive YOUR car ahead an inch and be sure it was only an inch? Homer could.)

Bob Marvil's signals to Homer were determined by what barriers loomed before the house, and by the actions of another remarkable man, George Shelton, who was balancing himself precariously on the steep roof of the house. The old roof shingles of the Camp Meeting house kept crumbling and falling to the pavement below The house inched forward. And there was George up there on the roof, slinging a hundred-pound traffic light up and over and out of the way. The light kept changing from red to yellow to green to red to yellow to green in a frightening automaton way. Traffic piled up. Spectators were frozen to rigid attention. Straining, George lifted the double tiers of lights around himself, and struggling to keep his footing, inched the lights along to the back end of the moving house.

When the traffic lights were finally swinging wildly but safely behind him, George returned to the front of the peaked roof. He squatted on the narrow pinnacle, thrust his leg into the air before him, and with his foot pulled up four heavy wires, one at a time. Somehow, he raised these until he had two of them under each arm. He then straightened up slowly, and, moving like a tight rope artist, balanced along the house-top until he could release the cables safely behind the house. He then returned forward, ready to meet the next threat. A biting cold wind was blowing, but George was panting and sweating.

Down below, the onlookers' hearts had gone up in their throats. As George wiped his forehead and sank down for a second of rest, breathing resumed among the sidewalk engineers and they regained enough strength to applaud heartily.

Perchance you may decide to move your house one day. If, however, you have a heart problem or anything, it might be best for you to take in a movie or engage in other diversion while the action is on. When you return, there your house will be, tidy and shipshape, and snugly sitting on its new site. You can then smile happily and say, "There's life in the old house, yet".

One thing is certain. If he had ever met the Sussex County Marvil brothers, Mohammed wouldn't have had that problem with the mountain.

EIGHT

The Long White Line

All men have favorite sitting spots, probably. My husband, Ward, has a beauty. It begins, as masculine nooks often do, with a big, sinky chair and foot stool. This upholstered nucleus is flanked on one side by a long, wide window sill whose paint bears witness to having supported many a cup of tea or coffee. On the other side is gathered an assortment of small tables. A few short steps away are desk, typewriter, and filing cabinets. Within easy tossing distance is a wastepaper basket full of crumpled discards, and surrounded by a straggly ring of papery crinkles which haven't quite hit the bull's eye.

All flat surfaces in this jumbled maze are piled high with pads of lined paper, reference books, cracked and handle-less mugs full of pencils, saucers with Gem razor blades to keep the pencils sharp, a battered Tahitian dictionary, dishes of paper clips, and a drift of bulging Manila folders, the arrangement of which suggests they were tossed there by a high wind.

All of this myriad of items is SACROSANCT and not to be touched by ANYBODY. Consequently, that section of the room hasn't been dusted in years. Heaven only knows what lost treasures are buried beneath the debris.

Such a masculine raven's nest of flotsam, jetsam, peace,

and security is probably repeated in many households. What makes Ward's anchorage unique, however, is its location -- right next to a large second-floor window which commands a superb view. In the foreground lies Silver Lake. In the background stretches the Atlantic Ocean. From this crow's nest in winter, the eye raised from work can watch hundreds of Canada geese and ducks on the lake, or note that a northeast wind is sending gigantic waves over the dunes which roll between the lake and the ocean. In summer, one's concentration is diverted by little sailboats dashing about the lake. On gusty days, many of these provide drama by dumping their navigators into the shallow water. Out on the ocean, enormous tankers and other vessels raise their bulks against the horizon while plying to or from Wilmington and Philadelphia, situated to the north up the Delaware River.

From this favorite spot, one October, Ward's voice suddenly cut into the morning quiet. "Come and take a look! There's the weirdest thing out there on the ocean!"

I rushed upstairs. It WAS weird. Stretching about a block long, a thick, turbulent white line of something was moving slowly and steadily southward along the coast.

"What do up suppose it is?" Ward said. "Birds? Big white birds of some kind?"

Looking at it through the binoculars didn't help any. Individual spots all along the line seemed in constant motion, giving the appearance of large birds beating their wings. The spots seemed to seethe and change location, but the long line itself moved with great stability in an unwavering southward course.

65

Ward shook his head. "Can't be birds. Nothing is flying into the air. Must be a big school of fish or something."

As we watched, the line slowly disappeared behind the houses at the south end of Silver Lake. Our strong desire was to hop in the car in pursuit of this enigma. Reluctantly, however, we were forced to leave the mystery unsolved. An appointment kept us from rushing to the beach to get a better look.

The unusual sight lingered in our minds, however. Not too long afterward, we ran into a retired Rear Admiral friend, and asked him about the long white line. This old salt knew right away what the line was. It wasn't birds or fish, he said, going on to explain that water moving away from the shore meets water moving toward the shore, thus forming a rip current. When this situation is combined with a wind blowing obliquely toward shore, the result is the long line of boiling foam, which travels with the wind direction just beyond the breaker line.

So that was that. But not too many days later, there the line was again, long, white, and impressive, and as before, traveling southward as if nothing could stop it. A native resident of Rehoboth stopped in about this time, noticed the unusual formation, and asked if we knew what it was. We gave him the Admiral's explanation, but even that did not seem to satisfy him.

"Maybe you ought to write a little squib about it," Ward said to me. "Lots of people must have seen it and would be interested. You'd have to do some research, of course."

So it was off to the books. And what a work-out! In the index of the Encyclopedia Britannica, under "Ocean" there are thirty-three listings covering everything from "Animal Life" to "Whirlpools". The sum total of these learned pieces spreads over hundreds of pages, and would take the good part of a lifetime to digest. The article on "Tides" alone stretches out for fourteen double-column, fine-print large pages, not to mention ten pages on "Oceanography" and another ten on "Waves and Shore Currents". The whole mind-boggling thing is full of graphs and diagrams and sentences like "The usual procedures for dealing with short waves in water is to solve the hydronamic equations of motion and the equation of continuity for an incompressible medium . . ."

Good Grief!

PhD's up to their water-wings in ocean terminology might be able to understand what the Enc. Brit. was talking about, but it left this aging land lubber feeling stupid, uneducated, and thwarted.

"It's Greek to me," Ward said. "But you'll have to come up with some sort of scientific explanation about that long white line. It's so dramatic."

He pointed to a section of the "Wave" article. "It says there that the following is a simple solution. Why don't you quote that?"

Okay. Here is what it said.

$$\phi = \frac{gH}{2\sigma}e^{ks}\cos(kx - \sigma t)$$

Does that make everything clear?

NINE

The Delaware Moors

Almost everybody visiting or living in this area has heard about the Delaware Moors. These distinctive groups of people of mysterious origin live in two principal locations in the state -- around Indian River in Sussex County, and in the vicinity of Cheswold, west of Dover, in Kent County.

To the best of anyone's knowledge, these Delaware settlements of Moors, plus two others, are the only such groups of people on the Eastern Seaboard. In addition to the Indian River and Cheswold communities, a splinter group exists in New Jersey. Another group lives in South Carolina.

This latter colony was the subject of an article which appeared in the *New York Times* in 1953 entitled "The Turks of Sumter County". This story stated that the existence of a self-contained but mysterious group of people had been recognized in South Carolina as far back as the 18th Century. It went on to quote from the 1790 Journals of the House of Representatives of South Carolina containing a report about the unique community living in the state, which officially recognized this community by saying that "persons who are subjects of the Emperor of Morocco are free in this state". In the 1790 Journal, these people were referred to as "the free Moors".

This *New York Times* article of 1953 continued by saying that for centuries the group had kept itself apart from other races, but that recently (the free Moors) "have regretted their clannishness and have tried to integrate".

As does any other nationality, Delaware's Moors, as well as those in South Carolina, have a variety of physical characteristics. Their skin color varies from white to the tan everybody strives to achieve on summer beaches. The majority of them have straight black hair, but some among them have sandy, blonde, or red hair. Eye color can be brown, grey, or blue. Their noses are most often straight and chiseled, and their lips are thin. Many of them belong to the Methodist Episcopal Church, and have maintained their own places of worship, usually engaging a white minister.

Who are the Moors, and how did they get to Delaware? These two questions have intrigued archaeologists and historians for centuries, and much has been written about them. C. A. Weslager, the noted Delaware historian, devoted a book to exploring these questions entitled *Delaware's Forgotten Folk -- The Story of the Moors and Nanticokes.*

Over the years, these proud people have struggled to preserve their identity, but their efforts have been uphill work. The difficulties they have faced were perhaps summed up by an article written for the *Philadelphia Times* in 1892. In it, a Moor from the Cheswold area was quoted as saying, "Sixty years ago, everyone knew who and what we were. No one ever thought of confusing us with any other race. But people around here are all newcomers. They know nothing about us and have never troubled their heads to inquire. They don't know any better." (Note: Eighty-five years later, there are still few people who trouble to inquire.)

In spite of this prevailing attitude, there has been some acknowledgement of Moors as Moors. The use of "Moor" as a race has been used on birth certificates, draft questionnaires, and other official documents, often inconsistently. Until very recently, the State of Delaware recognized Moors as an ethnic unit on Drivers' Licenses. Current drivers' permits ignore "race" in their descriptions. But up until late 1975, Delaware listed race codes on the backs of all drivers' licenses. Among these were separate listings for Negro, Oriental, Red, White, and Moor.

Abolishing these distinctions on current licenses is obviously intended to be part of the national integration effort. Whether or not this blending of all nationalities will succeed is beyond the scope of this chapter. However, it is interesting to note that at the same time great strides are being taken toward the goal of integration, there has also arisen among various ethnic groups a renewed sense of pride in their separateness and in their origins. Also gaining strength has been the desire to preserve the traditions which make each ethnic group unique.

Although it would seem to be an apparent dichotomy of aim, this trend is apparent all over the country. Rather than striving to have everybody blend into a "oneness", Indians now want to preserve their cultural heritage and be Indians. Blacks are proud of being Black. Spanish Americans want to emphasize their Spanishness; Poles, their Polishness, and so on.

Will Delaware's Moors be able to preserve the traditions and a sense of their history which make them so unique? Probably not, but it is remarkable that the Moors have been able to maintain their separate identity as long as they have. In their efforts to remain Moors, much has been against them. Census takers and other officials have rarely bothered to make a distinction between Moors and other races. Even their attempts to educate their children as Moors have been thwarted. For years, Sussex County Moor children in the Indian River Hundred attended their own school, the Harmon School. In 1921, the Delaware Legislature recognized the existence of this school by stating: "The State Board of Education may establish schools for the children of people called 'Moors'. No white or colored child shall be permitted to attend such a school . . ."

For a time, children of both Moor and Nanticoke heritage attended this school. Then the Nanticoke Indians decided to withdraw from the Harmon School and built another exclusively for the use of children of Nanticoke Indian descent -- the Indian Mission School. At the same time, there were also nearby schools for white children and for black children. So the Delaware Legislature again swung into action with a law which stated that "The State Board of Education may establish schools for children of people called Moors or Indians . . ." Later, they passed another law which said "No white or colored child shall be permitted to attend any school for Moors or any school for Indians . . ."

Obviously, both Moors and Indians were fighting hard to keep themselves as separate races. But all this came to naught in the 1960's, when, under Federal Law, all such ethnic schools were closed and forced to integrate. During the school struggle, however, and even before that, there had been intermarriage between Moors and Nanticokes, and gradually the distinction between the two races has dimmed. As the *Delaware Guide* of 1938 said: "The social lines these people draw among themselves often baffle their white neighbors and the State authorities alike. Though the Delaware school system is officially divided into white and Negro schools, there are four separate kinds in this Indian River Hundred region."

As a matter of fact, people in the Indian River Community who might once have considered themselves as Moors have now almost completely identified themselves as Nanticoke Indians. Over the years, both the Moors and the Nanticokes struggled to establish and maintain their separate ethnic identities as distinct from both whites and blacks. With help from the Federal Government and from the many interested people who have come to do research in the community, the Nanticokes were greatly more successful in this than were the Moors. In the fifty-five years since the Nanticoke Indian Association was established in the Indian River Community, the organization has gained strength and importance.

In 1977, for instance, a *"Photographic Survey of Indian River Community"* was published as an "initial step in achieving a sense of identity" for the Nanticokes. In October of that same year, the first Pow Wow in many years was held, complete with Indian costumes, dances, songs, and "fried bread" -- a dish similar to corn pone. An estimated number of seven hundred people attended the event, and it was such a huge success that there are plans to repeat the Pow Wow annually.

Because of these Nanticoke achievements, and also because of the widespread intermarriage between the two races over the centuries, it seems only natural that the Moors as Moors have blended into the Nanticokes of the Indian River. In *Delaware's Forgotten Folk*, Mr. Weslager calls the Moors "mixed bloods". And it is interesting to note that some of the families he named as Moors -- Sammons, Johnson, Carter, Corney -- are well represented in the 1977 Nanticoke Indian Association publication. In the Cheswold community of Moors, the identification of Moors with Indians has not occurred to any such extent.

But however blurred the issue, it can be accepted as fact that in Southern Delaware there exist people whose blood lines go back to Morocco.

And so we are back to the question, "How did the Moors get here?" Over the years, three principal theories have been put forth in an attempt to pierce the mystery surrounding the Delaware Moors' origins. In *Delaware's Forgotten Folk*, Weslager discusses these three legends:

The Pirate Legend

This theory about the Moors' origins holds that prior to the Revolution, Moorish pirates were shipwrecked off the southern coast of Delaware. The pirates were rescued by the Nanticoke Indians. After a while, the pirates married Nanticoke women and brought up families. Their descendants became the people known as Moors.

73

The Romantic Legend

This tradition, with many variations, states that a wealthy Spanish woman, Senorita Requa, lived near Lewes on a large plantation. She purchased a handsome slave who was African. Versions differ as to his original nationality. Some stories even make him a Moorish Prince. Eventually, Senorita Requa and "the Prince" married. Their children intermarried with the Nanticoke Indians, and their descendants became the Moors.

In 1855, Lydia Clark, a Nanticoke Indian, supported this legend by testimony she gave in a court trial held in Georgetown, Delaware. (Lydia Clark's memory was honored in 1927 by the Society of Colonial Dames, who erected a monument to her at Oak Orchard, citing her as the last of the Nanticoke Indians in Delaware to speak the Indian tongue.) The purpose of the trial was to establish the original nationality of a defendant named Isaiah Harmon.

As Weslager notes, several things become peculiarly interesting on reading the accounts of this trial, particularly the glaring omission in Lydia Clark's testimony of the use of the word "Moor". Never once did she use this term, even though the designation "Moor" was then in widespread use throughout Delaware. And, as Weslager also says, it is clear that many forces were at work at the time to compel all Moorish and Indian descendants to deny their origins. For these and other reasons, Lydia Clark's people maintained after her death that she was pressured into giving her testimony, and that her story had no basis of truth in it.

The Colonial Legend

This story states that before the Revolution, a group of Moors sailed to this country to found a colony. The colonists intermarried with the Nanticokes, and lived in their own settlements. Writing about this theory, Weslager says, "There seems to be no historical basis to support this tale."

Thus, with a wave of his second chapter, did Weslager dismiss the Colonial Legend. Since the publication of *Delaware's Forgotten Folk,* however, a new theory has come to light. Material has been unearthed which strongly supports the Colonial Legend, in which the Moors arrived in this country as colonizers. It comes from research done by Donald Downs of Aspendale, Down's Chapel, Kent County, Delaware,

Drawing by Catherine Tanzer

who has been a student of Delaware history all of his life. His house, Aspendale, was built in 1771. The lovely old building has now been declared an historic monument, and is one of the few Delaware houses which have always remained in the ownership of descendants of the original builders. Aspendale is situated close by Cheswold, where the Kent County Moors have been settled for centuries, and Donald Downs' grandfather built near Aspendale the first schoolhouse to be used exclusively by the Moors of that area.

Donald grew up knowing about Moors, as for over two hundred years, Moors have worked in and around Cheswold in numerous occupations, have farmed there, and many have been tenant farmers on Aspendale land, and still are.

In 1938, Donald Downs visited for several months a cousin of his who lived in Tangier, Morocco. While there, he met Maxwell Blake, the American Consul General in Tangier, considered an outstanding historian of Tangier. As the friendship developed, Mr. Blake learned of Donald's interest in the origins of the Delaware Moors. He told Donald a story he had discovered through research. Donald later corroborated much of the story from files in the British Museum, and placed the full account in the State Archives Building in Dover. Here is the story, which strongly supports the Colonization legend.

A Fourth Theory about the Moors' Origin

In 1662, Charles II of England married the Portuguese Princess, Catherine of Braganza. As part of her dowry, Catherine brought under English possession the seaport of

Tangier, Morocco. To police Tangier, England sent out a regiment, commanded by General Piercy Kirke, known as "Kirke's Lambs".

Throughout the time of British control, there were numerous uprisings against British occupation. In 1684, because of the increasing expense of defending Tangier, England decided to withdraw her troops. The following sequel to this decision is a quotation from the account of Mr. Blake:

"When England decided to give up Tangier and did so in 1684, a number of the younger companies of 'Kirke's Lambs' decided to go to America, and set sail in that year, taking with them Moorish women. They landed in America on an island in the Chesapeake Bay, *and named it Tangier Island, for the country from which they had come.* (The italics are mine.) However, these Moors remained a very short time on Tangier Island, moving to Sussex and Kent Counties, Delaware."

In his report filed in Dover, Donald Downs comments further:

"From the above verbal report by Maxwell Blake, the Moors of Delaware are descended from the English members of Kirke's Lambs and the Moorish women they brought to America. This explains the predominating English names of the Moors of Kent County -- Morgan, Ridgway, Beckett, Moseley, Dean, Durham, Carney, Carey, Seeney, etc.

"Some of the Moors who went to Sussex County intermarried with the Nanticoke Indians, and some of the ones who came to Kent County may also have married with Indians, but predominantly they married among themselves, as they still do today."

77

Donald's comments on the English names of the Kent County Moor families apply as well to many Sussex County Moor families -- names such as Wright, Harmon, Street, and others. Clark, Johnson, and Norwood names are now considered as Nanticoke Indians, but this well might have been a result of intermarriage between the two races.

About the Moors, Weslager says, "If we could turn back the calendar . . . seventy-five years, we should find many of the ancient customs persisting strongly and almost universally observed by all (Moor) families. The . . . twentieth century is changing the thoughts, customs, and industries of the Moors. The old is gradually being replaced by the new."

The Moors and the Nanticokes of Indian River and of Cheswold remain a vital part of the story of early Delaware, and, indeed, of today's Delaware. These unique communities reach into the early history of the southern part of the state. In our concentration on things modern, let us hope that the story of the Moors, this interesting footnote to history, will not be lost forever. And certainly it should be remembered that the Indian River Moors and Nanticoke Indians add much to the interest and variety which exist in Sussex County.

II

THE SEASONS

TEN

Sussex In The Spring

Spring, "with her golden suns and silver rains" is the most glorious of seasons. In variety and excitement, spring is equalled only by summer, autumn, and winter. Which point of view is not meant to down-grade spring in the least - - - merely to spread the applause equally among every day of the year. After all, even if you live to be eighty, you are only going to experience three hundred and twenty seasons, and that's not nearly enough time to explore all their themes and variations. So there's no sense in playing favorites.

Spring is inspiring, though. Flirtatious and unpredictable, maybe, but marvelous withal. In Sussex County, spring usually decides to put in an initial appearance about mid-March. Often, however, winter, who has been sulking about being pushed off center stage, decides to roar in for a brief return engagement, blowing frostily on the new buds and snowing all over the daffodils.

But in a few weeks, the spring palette begins to splash color across the dark winter canvas. To watch this succession of spring blossoms in Sussex is like experiencing a touchable rainbow. First come the snowdrops, the hyacinths, and the crocuses. These are followed by joyous bursts of yellow in the daffodils and forsythia. Complementing these golden smiles are the blues of periwinkle, the soft pinks and reds of the flowering fruit trees and the redbuds, the lavendars of the lilacs, the dazzling whites of dogwood and narcissus.

Early in this rhythmic progression, trees which have shivered leafless through the winter send tender shoots into the warming days. There seems to be no word in English to describe precisely the color of these emerging leaves, but their appearance transforms Delmarva's scattered groves of trees into billowing veils of green chiffon, richly embroidered and laced with dogwood blossoms.

As it blossoms, each plant pours out its own profusion of heady scent, enabling every dancing breeze to carry along the intoxicating perfumes of flowering spring.

Dogwood

Gradually, the early spring palette gives way to the lush reds and pinks of the azaleas, the deep blues and purples of iris and ajuga, and everywhere the exhuberant cascades of spiraea.

As these glories begin to fade, the first blossoms of rhododendron begin to spread their petals to the sun, mock orange fills the air with sweetness, peony and clematis buds swell. Soon the velvet colors of roses will spill over fences and send their heavy redolence through the cutting gardens. Then, leaf by deepening leaf, spring's newness will yield to the hot, sweet intensity of summer.

A special early spring delight occurs when clouds of white flowers suddenly appear against the dark evergreens bordering the lakes and marshy areas. These beautiful mass exhibits of star-like blossoms are staged by the shadbush, a member of the rose family and a native North American shrub. The shadbush is among the earliest of the wild flowering plants, producing its profusion of bloom "when the shad run", as tradition has it. In Sussex County, shadbush is a tall, full shrub, opening its flowers in advance of the leaves. In other locations across the country, shadbush varieties can grow to a height of sixty or seventy feet.

Shadbush is also variously known as shadblow, serviceberry, and June berry. In addition, it has a Latin name, though it seems a shame for anything as lacily graceful as shadblow to be weighted down with a monicker like *Amelanchier Canadensis*.

At the same time *Amelanchier Canadensis* is doing its thing,

Forsythia is spreading cascades of yellow-gold all over the place. Also brightening the landscape are *Tulipa Suaveolens, Narcissus Bulbocodium, Prunus Subhirtella,* and *Vincae* . . . oh, forget it! Enough of this botanical Latinizing. What romance would there be left in the world if people went around murmuring into a loved one's ear

> Rosae Wichuraianae are red
> Erythonia Dencanis are blue
> Hybrid Saccharum Robustum and Beta
> Vulgaris are sweet
> And so are you.

Shadblow

Spring is a marvelous time to become again aware of the inter-relations of all earthly things. To observe this, you have only to look out your window. In your yard, bees and humming birds sip the nectar of azaleas. Song sparrows search the grass for delectable weeds. Small, white-tailed rabbits nibble contentedly on long sprays of forysthia leaves. Robins run across the lawn, listening for the faint squiggles of bugs and worms. Butterflies search among the tulips and ajuga for food. (Did you know, incidentally, that not all butterflies are silent? Some species emit shrill chirping notes. Others make clicking sounds. That's what it says in the book, anyway. How would it be as a conversational opener? "I heard the most intriguing butterfly song today.")

As they nibble or peck or sip their dinners, most of these wild things are also involved in re-creating through pollination, the plants they are eating. Renewal and re-birth also hang heavy in the air as the pine trees release their pollen into the spring

breezes. (If quantity of wind-blown pollen deposit were the only factor involved in a pine tree's reproduction, our living room furniture and floors would each year produce a vast forest of pines.)

House sparrows seem to respond to spring by getting awfully proprietary about everything. These population exploders have claimed as Sparrow City the ivy which clambers over the outside of our house, originally planted there in a vain attempt to camouflage the 1923 stucco facade. The sparrows also think that an upstairs window air conditioner was mounted there especially for sparrow-nesting purposes. Each spring, one more happy family of sparrows chirps to maturity in this air conditioner, thus not only interfering with any desire we might have to cool off the room on a hot spring day, but also adding even more hungry sparrow mouths to our yard's bird population, already top heavy with house sparrows.

Throughout each lengthening day, the sparrows search the ground for nest-building materials. For birds of such a lowly reputation, they display great persnicketiness in their choice of structural components. This long piece of string will be just right. That pine chat is not worth picking up. Frequently, two or more of them argue heatedly over who is entitled to a particularly desirable fragment. A furious feathered tug-of-war ensues. The combatants voice their claims with ear-splitting cheeps. Wings beat menacingly. Intimidating leaps into the air are made. Finally, the victor wrests the prize from the beak of his rival, and retreats quickly under the shrubbery bearing his bit of lacey weed or long string of wild sweet pea vine.

Sooner or later, this flotsam is woven into one of the dozens of nests which lean out of our ivy in bedraggled loops. And in a little while, the sparrow population will have again doubled, tripled, quadrupled, out-numbering other birds by the dozens. Ah, well!

In addition to having swallows in the ivy, we also have swifts in the chimney. (Having bats in the belfry is just around the corner. Or already upon us.)

Each year, an apparently enormous family of chimney swifts is brooded, hatched and fed in a nest attached to the side of our chimney flue. This means that on every food-bringing visit of the parents, the nestlings' chattering and peeping is so loud it drowns out all conversation in the living room. The uproar is so tremendous, visitors think the nest is located right on top of the damper. But perhaps the chimney acts as an amplifier, magnifying the cheeps to their double-decibel intensity. During these times of ordeal, invitations to our house always read, "Come and listen to our chimney."

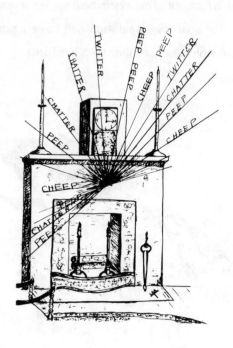

Humanwise, the reaction to the end of winter is not necessarily so uproarious, but it is equally wondrous.

On almost any warm day in this area, when the salt tang of the ocean travels on a gentle breeze through sunlit afternoons, you can spot a couple of people settling themselves comfortably on one of the sidewalk benches scattered around Rehoboth.

"Watching the world go by," one will say, sipping happily on a coke. Radiating from both the loiterers will be a delight in the situation of the moment -- the beauty of the day, the savoring of a simple pleasure, the joy in being able to sit unmolested, relishing a perfect small moment in time.

"There aren't many places left today where you can find this," the other will say.

There aren't either. Here in this yet unspoiled spot, the spring air blows fresh and the rhythms of life still beat slowly, in tune with the revolving earth.

ELEVEN

Summer At The Shore.......
Color It Crowded

When it's summer near the ocean
There is far too much commotion:
No parking places on the street,
You cannot find a place to eat

Without a crowd outside, unable
To be seated at a table.
Before you land in such congestion,
Take Maalox for your indigestion.

From mid-June on, in this resort,
It's hard to buy a steak, or quart
Of milk, because the hungry throng
Jams super-markets all day long.

To purchase just one little peach
Takes hours in mobbed Rehoboth Beach.
And, as you watch the milling pack
You feel that something's gone off track.

If people pour in more and more
Will we have lost what they came for?
Are shopping lines, ad nauseum
Just what they're all escaping from?

Will grumblers put up signs, "Beware
The crowds in Coastal Delaware"?
Will tourists pick up stakes and flee
To towns with more tranquillity?

Will trippers want to pack their bags
And head for *Boros* --- *Gum* or *Dags*?
Will they cheer and cry "Hosanna!"
On reaching Millville or Roxana?

Or will they even (What a pity!)
Decide to go back to the city?
"At last," they'll say, "A quiet place
With lots of room and breathing space.

"And yet we seem to miss the shore.
We miss the sand, the ocean's roar.
There may be mobs and great commotion
But still we hanker for that ocean.

"Alas we wouldn't trade that spot
For any other, crowds or not.
"There's room enough," Rehoboth means
Be you old or in your teens."

So they'll come back the next weekend
But now each person brings a friend
Along, because there's no place more
Delicious than the Sussex Shore.

TWELVE

Summer .... *Legs, Legs, Legs*

Generally speaking, the costumes people wear in summer are enough to plunge all lovers of beauty into deepest gloom.

All winter long, various eyesores and minor deformities have been mercifully hidden under layers of concealing garments. But, in summer, out come the minis, the short shorts, the bikinis, the halter tops. And there, for all the world to see are the rolls, the bulges, and the ungirdled hips.

Also exposed to the shrinking eye of the observer are the knobs and angles of men's legs, which frequently rise hairily out of brown winter oxfords and drooping, mid-calf socks. The masculine topside view is often not much better. Puny men always seem to embrace sleeveless, net T-shirts with low, round necks against which a few straggly hairs nestle. Paunchy, bay-windowed gentlemen go in for loud, flowered shirts which billow over violently striped shorts. To top off these sartorial sins, the men add crowning glories of large, Texas-style straw hats, or jaunty caps with eyelet holes everywhere, or "les chapeaux sportifs" --- straw numbers laden with golf tees, fishing flies, or, if you can believe it, miniature beer cans.

Most noticeably assymetrical, however, are legs, legs, legs. There seem to be no readily available statistics on American limbs, gams, extremeties, shanks, pins. Call them what you will, a conservative guess is that only one out of every ten thousand people possesses legs at all worth looking at, and that only one woman in a hundred thousand should flash them around à la Marlene Dietrich. What have we done to deserve all the other 99,999 pairs forced on our reluctant eyesight? Most legs, young or old, male or female, are too thin, too fat, bowed, knobby, knock-kneed, thick, shapeless, veined, hairy, bulbous, or otherwise inelegant.

A dominant thrust of human progress from the time of primeval ooze to the present has been toward the beautification of the ugly. One way to accomplish this is to cover up unsightly bulges. Besides, a little mystery always lends allurement, no?

If you have any questions about all this, head for any resort at the height of the season. The summer sights will astound and amaze you.

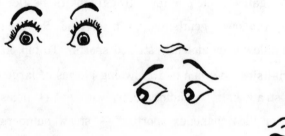

THIRTEEN

Summer .... *Operation Speckles*

Vacationers in Sussex often experience the kind of small happening which imprints the summer with indelible memories.

Such a souvenir was presented one year to a young couple named Robert and Lynn Wilson, to their neighbors, their neighbor's house guests, and their own and the neighbor's dogs. "Operation Speckles", they called it.

One July day, the Wilson's son, Andy, age nine, found an apparently abandoned and dying baby Robin in the yard. Picking it up carefully, he rushed to show his parents. They all looked at it feeling overwhelmed and wondering what to do next. The baby bird's heart was beating, but his eyes were closed, and he had the sad, bedraggled look of a "goner".

Being a bird lover of some experience, Lynn Wilson felt that the parent Robins might still be nearby. But before putting the baby outside again, she fed him some gruel and water with an eye dropper. Baby Speckles, as he was soon dubbed because of the juvenile spots on his breast, responded to this treatment, begging with open mouth for more, and seeming to gain strength after several feedings.

Hoping the parents would return, the Wilsons placed Speckles in a low box in the yard. At this point, the Wilson's dog, Inky, part Labrador, apparently decided Speckles was her responsibility. She placed herself on guard near Speckles' box, growling ominously when strangers or stray cats came near. By nightfall, no parent Robins had appeared, so Speckles was brought inside, Inky following closely behind.

Meantime, the Wilson's neighbors found themselves also happily embroiled in Operation Speckles. This new group of Robin foster parents included a grandmother, her married children, various grandchildren, and two house guests. These guests had once raised a baby Mockingbird, and proved to be an invaluable source of information on the complex needs of baby-bird-raising. Also in on the act was the neighbor's poodle, Martha, who decided it was her natural right to join Inky in mothering this odd looking but appealing new puppy.

Presently Operation Speckles was clicking along efficiently. Somebody came up with an enormous bird cage, with lots of

Speckles

perches and plenty of hopping room. Tiny, beak-size balls were made of peanut butter plus soy bean oil, plus ground vitamins and yeast, plus bird seed. Grapes were peeled. Currants and apples were purchased. Small dog food was crushed into Robin-sized pieces. Fishermen's worms were chopped into baby-bird mouthfuls.

Speckles flourished under all this Tender Loving Care. He learned to sit on fingers, arms, and shoulders for feeding. He uttered gratifying little thank-you squeaks. He enjoyed regular practice periods of hopping and flying on the screen porch. He fluffed out, and his tail feathers grew.

Throughout this phase, Inky constantly maintained guard position, rarely venturing more than a foot away from her foster child. When Inky did feel it necessary to absent herself from Speckles, Martha took over the guardianship. Frequently, when Inky decided Speckles was hopping too far afield, Inky took the bird gently in her mouth, Labrador fashion, and returned him to box or cage. Speckles seemed to think this a normal procedure.

Inky drooled a lot during this operation, however, either from excitement or love. As a result, the Wilsons found themselves spending long hours washing saliva from Speckles' feathers, and discouraged Inky's charming but drippy means of transportation.

As Speckles grew, he was taken outside each day. There, he was tossed into the air to try his wings. Time after time, he fluttered to the ground, where he was quickly guarded by Inky, and subsequently returned to his cage.

One Sunday, however, about a month after he had been

rescued, Speckles spent almost the entire day eating voraciously, and preening and grooming his feathers. On Monday, when he was taken for his outdoor exercise, he came into Robin maturity, and flew from the outstretched hands to a nearby tree limb.

Everybody watched breathlessly while this growing-up process took place. Speckles fluttered from branch to nearby branch, chirping a lot, and looking toward his large group of ground-bound admirers. Higher and higher in the trees Speckles rose. Finally, with strong and steady wing-beat, Speckles flew away.

For weeks, Speckles' adopted family searched the sky and trees for sight of their foundling. He never returned. And although they all felt the world was a little emptier without him, all foster parents could only hope that Speckles had made a successful re-entry into his natural sphere. In any event, Speckles had forever made himself a niche in the chambers of their minds where warm memories are collected.

FOURTEEN

Summer.......
Down The Garden Path

To many people, gardening and summer are synonymous. To others of us, alas, gardening is a sometime thing.

Sometime means April, May, and June.

During those sparkling months, we are consumed by "The Spirit of Gardening". It becomes impossible to pass a garden shop without stopping "just to see what they have". Fatal move! Once inside these emporia, the long aisles of little seedlings become as irresistible as puppies in a pet shop window. They smile up at us, begging us to buy them. Our imagination goes crazy. Visions of sensational flower beds, riotous with color, fill our mind's eye. We picture ourselves, cool and gracious, strolling through long stretches of blossoms nodding gently in the summer breeze.

Fired by these dreams, we thrust aside our inner whisperings of caution and load the car with flat after flat of this and that allurement. Wait! We really do need something for that bare spot near the bird bath. How about a couple or three or more of those fat round shrubs, so neat and thriving in their burlap coverings?

Why not? So it is home with all these goodies. Later, there are more trips back for fertilizer and other items to enrich both the soil and the garden shop proprietor. And the springtime weeks that follow are filled with bird song, euphoria, dream gardens, and the faint smell of manure.

Then along come July and August, the sweat, bug, and weed months. As the summer sun scorches across the sizzling sky, the very thought of putting trowel to dirt makes us feel faint. We droop in front of fan or air conditioner, sipping listlessly at iced tea. As we languish, our once bright fantasies of garden glory melt into the reality of conquest by tall and vigorous weeds. "Survival of the weediest," we call it.

So, around our house, has it been and probably ever will be. And over the years, we have come to accept the bitter fact that our green thumbs turn brown and sere under the hot summer sun. Every dark truth has its silver wisdom, however, and the awareness of our spring ups and summer downs has always kept us from succumbing to the temptation of putting in a vegetable garden.

Except for one year, that is. In that fatal early spring, the ruinous price-tag on a head of cauliflower finally managed to tumble the walls of our resistance. The vegetable garden worm turned, as it were. If others can produce green garden plots of luscious vegetables, why can't we? And how marvelous it will be, we mused, to wander through the fruitful fields, to gather baskets of flavorful tomatoes, to heap the apron full of sweet green beans and crisp peppers, and to watch the cantaloupes swelling into juicy ripeness. How thrifty! How basic! How back to nature!

How deluded!

July came and went. August scorched in, and with it came --

again -- the knowledge that hopes, dreams, and seed-packets do not a vegetable gardener make. Our springtime reveries, alack, had not included the cabbage worm, the cut worm, the slug, the thrip, the spider mite, nor even yet, the white-tailed rabbit. All too late we learned that a cauliflower may be worth every penny of its budget-ruining price.

Let's see. How did it figure out, exactly?

Garden Expenses --- April to August 15

APRIL

Man to help dig	$24.00
Manure, lime, fertilizer, etc.	29.72
Plants and seeds	26.00

MAY

Replacements for trowel lost, trowel bent, pick-axe broken	11.49
New hose (Old one wasn't long enough)	6.75
Stakes and chicken wire for fence against rabbits	12.60
"No Nibble" spray for rabbits	2.49
Band-Aids for blisters, and 3 cans "Off" for mosquitoes	3.15
4 pkgs. spray for thrips, aphids, etc.	11.82
Therapy sessions at Beebe Hospital for bad back	60.00

JUNE

Six-pack beer to kill slugs	1.85
Man to weed because of bad back	20.00

JULY

Man to weed because of heat and bad back.

Also spray for bugs	24.00
More beer for slugs	1.85
More spray for spider mites	5.96

AUGUST

Forget it!

Grim total	$241.68

A sizeable chunk of moolah. And if you harbor the notion that in spite of all expense and weary bones, we at least found ourselves singing the joyous songs of harvest and heaping high the cornucopias of plenty, think again.

By mid-August, our entire crop consisted of (1) Two wizened heads of cauliflower. (Not only were they wizened, they were also LAVENDER! Our taste buds went into a decline.) (2) 16 string beans, harvested, fortunately, before the spider mites arrived. (3) 2 stalks of broccoli. (These took advantage of our inexperienced ways with vegetables and burst into brilliant yellow bloom before we got around to picking them. Taste buds again dismayed.) (4) Six peppers. (Four of these had funny-looking white slashes on them. (5) Zero cantaloupes, radishes, beets, and lettuce. (They all succumbed to some unknown but lethal blight.) and (6) Thirty-two tomatoes. (The spider-mites finally got them, too. Or was it the spray for the spider mites?)

All in all, we figured that made the major part of our edible crop --- the six peppers and the thirty-two tomatoes --- cost $6.32 apiece. Every string bean was worth eight cents each. Beside which, they were tough.

So, on August 15th, it was back to the super-market. Casting food-budget aside, we bought a cauliflower. It was gloriously white, and anything but wizened.

FIFTEEN

Summer.......
Cool Cucumbers And Hot Peppers

As that "Summer-of-the-vegetable-garden" wore on, we discovered that one man's heat may be a cucumber's Paradise.

Unveiled to our novice eyes was the fact that when the mercury soars and humidity wet-blankets the air, all the members of the cucumber and pepper families think that at long last some decent weather has arrived. As befits botanical immigrants from the tropics of Asia, Africa, and South America, they gratefully spring into impressive growth, leafing, blossoming, and fruiting like crazy in the jungle temperatures.

Sauna-bath weather caused eggplants to swell into purple taste delights. Bell peppers suddenly decided to bear enough fruit to season a ton or two of salad. And given a heat wave, our zucchinis began to act as if they thought they were watermelons. One day, these squashes would be the size of the small, manageable little vegetables you buy in grocery stores. The next day, they had exploded into enormous balloon-like objects, fifteen to twenty inches long, four to five inches in diameter, and weighing five to six pounds. County Fair material.

Today, everybody takes a "Ho Hum, So What?" attitude toward the zucchini, and recently published dictionaries list the vegetable under "Z". But back in the years when our *Webster's Unabridged* and *Encyclopedia Britannica* were published, zucchinis, like avocados, were rarities known only to a chosen few gourmets. Consequently, neither our *Unabridged* nor the *Encyl. Brit.* has a "Zucchini" listing. You have to look under "Squash", and the articles go on and on about gourds and pumpkins before they get around to mentioning that Vegetable Marrow and Zucchini are synonymous, and that they are members of the Cucurbitaceae family which has tropical origins. Cucumbers, gourds, squashes, pumpkins, and melons are all kissing cousins in this family, so maybe our out-size zucchinis had a bar sinister watermelon ancestor way back somewhere.

You might think that vegetables of such magnitude would be stringy and bitter. Not a bit of it! Sweet as honey and very tender. Slicing them, however, produced slabs as big as butter plates. Casting about for some way to cope with these Frisbees, we turned to a friend who has a cooking thumb and knows her way around the recipes. She gave us a marvelous way to serve zucchinis with middle-age spread. So here's a delectable dish made from zucchinis, middle-size to huge.

Stuffed Zucchini à la Mary Bolton

Simmer the whole zucchini until it is tender. (For huge ones, use a roasting pan.) Cool. Slice in half lengthwise. Scoop out the seeds. Sprinkle with salt and pepper. Mix together one egg, slightly beaten, one third cup cottage cheese, one cup shredded Cheddar cheese, chopped parsley, chives, salt, and pepper. Spread this mixture in the cavities. Bake fifteen minutes at 350 degrees, then turn oven to 450 for a few minutes until the stuffing is brown and bubbly.

Delectable! You might even say that one bite of this vegetarian ambrosia was worth the entire $241.68 April garden expenditure. Well, almost, anyway.

SIXTEEN

Summer.......
What Happened To All The Parsley?

Around Sussex, everyone is so used to seeing Monarch
butterflies, there is a tendency to take them as a natural part
of the summer day.

One mid-July, however, the sighting of a different kind of
large butterfly froze everybody at our house into positions of
watchful delight. Fluttering over our small herb and parsley
bed was a velvety black beauty with a wing spread of about
three and a half inches. Pale yellow polka dots formed a
brilliant edging along its forewings, merging into turquoise on
the hindwings. The butterfly was new to us and so
spectacular, we hardly dared to breathe.

After a few minutes of lingering on various parsley leaves,
the butterfly circled off. Later, in an effort to enlighten the
darkness of our total ignorance on butterflies, we searched
through books on "Lepidoptera", finally deciding that our
stunning visitor had been a Black Swallowtail, also called the
Common Eastern. (Common to others, maybe, but not to us.)

Little did we realize that day that this encounter would
launch us on one of those small series of events which serve to
open yet another window on the world. Three weeks passed,

during which we had only an occasional glad memory of our brilliant butterfly. One day in August, however, when we were showing our little herb garden to a friend, he suddenly said, "Good night! Look at all those huge caterpillars on your parsley!"

We looked. Busily chomping on parsley leaves were seven caterpillars about two inches long. But what caterpillars! It may seem odd to use the word "gorgeous" to describe creepy-crawlies who are munching steadily on your parsley. But that's the only word to use for those caterpillars. They were predominantly a vivid Van Gogh chartreuse color. Running around their bodies were ten or eleven jet black stripes, broken in a regular pattern of gold dots. Dior himself couldn't have dreamed up a more striking design.

"You can call them sensational all you want," our friend said, "but let me tell you something. In a couple of days, you're not going to have any parsley left." He reached over to pick them off.

"No! Please don't touch them!"

Our friend looked at us as if we were crazy. "What do you mean, you think they're your butterflies? They're caterpillars! And they're ruining your parsley!"

Yelling at him not to do anything, we rushed inside to consult the aforementioned butterfly books. Sure enough. The drawing of the Black Swallowtail larva looked just like the caterpillars on our parsley. Light dawned! When we had seen that beautiful butterfly back in July, she had been busy laying her eggs.

Our friend decided we had really lost our buttons when we

showed him the picture and announced we'd rather have Swallowtail butterflies than parsley any day.

Fired with new-born scientific enthusiasm, we put one of the parsley plants into a pot, gently transferred one of the caterpillars onto it, and brought the pot onto our sun porch.

"Rear Your Own Lepidoptera," the book urged us. "Caterpillars will pupate on twigs."

Why not? And so began our dip into the world of *Papilio polyxenes asterius*, the Latin name of our sun porch visitor. We spent hours in rapt observation of our specimen's eating habits. (Ravenous!) Our vocabularies expanded to include words like "larva" (the caterpillar stage) ; "pupa" (the caterpillar in a cocoon) ; "fritillary" (spotted butterflies) ; and "chrysalis" (the caterpillar after it sheds its skin and is inside the cocoon) . We learned there are one hundred and twenty thousand species of butterflies in the world, with about ten thousand in North America, and that butterflies have been around for seventy million years. Many species, like the Monarch, migrate great distances. Monarchs which flutter around this area in summer will spend the winter in Central Mexico. In their migrations, enormous clouds of butterflies have been spotted over the ocean, a thousand miles from their nearest known habitat. We also discovered that Swallowtails which have over-wintered in cocoons to emerge in the spring are quite different in appearance from summer butterflies produced from eggs laid the same season.

The big thrill --- "an awesome experience" --- the books said, was to witness the metamorphosis of a pupa into a butterfly. Our dreams were filled with visions of our butterfly coming out of its cocoon in slow motion, the way they do in nature films.

After two days on the sun porch, our caterpillar seemed to grow sluggish. He stopped eating and moving. "Maybe he's sick!" we thought. Several long, silky filaments seemed to be floating from his body.

He wasn't sick at all. Next morning, our larva had indeed changed himself into a pupa. All around himself he had spun a beautifully irridescent green cocoon, which was attached to the branch by a silken thread. The case was cleverly located on the under side of the parsley stem, and hard to spot under a cluster of the few remaining leaves. In the fork of the stem below him was a little ball, about an eighth of an inch in diameter, which was his discarded outer skin. You could still

see the green color and the black stripes on it.

The problem now was, how long did all this pupating go on before a butterfly emerged? A week? A month? All winter? We couldn't find the answer in any book. There was nothing to do but wait, making frequent, hopeful checks for a possible "awesome experience".

Meantime, back at the parsley bed, the caterpillars were indeed making it a ruin of leafless stems. Mama butterfly certainly had been busy. Tiny new larvae kept showing up. We learned to spot them when they were only about a sixteenth of an inch long. At that size, they were black, with a single white stripe around their bodies. As they grow, we read, they keep shedding their skins. When they are about three-quarters of an inch long, they are all black and white stripes, with lots of little protective spines sticking up around them. Their final handsome coloration looks a lot like sunlight through the leaves, and also serves as protection. And how they ate! The books neglect to tell you that one needs a SIZEABLE bed of Swallowtail food (parsley, carrots, celery, and parsnips) in order to have a successful Swallowtail hatchery. To keep our potential butterflies happy and content, we finally resorted to buying bunches of parsley at the grocery store. We put branches of it in little vials of water and buried them in the dirt.

Eight days after our sun porch caterpillar had spun its cocoon, we made a morning check. The cocoon seemed more irridescent, but otherwise no change, so we went off on errands. When we got back, we found an empty cocoon with the top agape.

Drat! Zounds! And other stronger expletives! We had missed the big moment!

But where was the butterfly! A little search found him quietly fanning his wings among the plants near the window. Our newly-emerged beauty was as jet black and as brilliantly spotted as the one seen in July. But this time, we were also able to notice his black and white striped body, the distinctive tails, and to see that the under-wings were a mottled orange.

Shortly we pushed the screen aside, and our porch-reared Swallowtail soared into the air, over the house, and away. We had missed the great moment of transformation, but at least we knew that out there somewhere was one more gorgeous Black Swallowtail to brighten the summer scene.

SEVENTEEN

Summer.......
An Onion Is A Miracle

There was this onion. He was raised in a Sussex County onion patch. The soil was to his liking --- light, nutritious, and carefully weeded. Sunshine poured chlorophyll into his greening leaves. The rains came, trickling through the surrounding earth to slake his thirst. By mid-summer, he had expanded his layers, and developed into a round, healthy bulb of pleasing dimensions.

On reaching this maturity, he was pulled from the carefree onion bed of his youth and laid on a rack to dry. The soft air moving around him gave his outside papery coat a tawny sheen. In due course, he was transported to a kitchen, which seems to be the unquestioned fate of so many onions.

Before long, most of him got cut off and put in a stew. The rest was thrust into a plastic bag and forgotten. There it sat in the onion basket getting more and more buried under mounds of whole and healthier onions.

Now the thing is, if most humans had been hacked at and stuffed into a smothering sack, they probably would have given up entirely. Even if they had clung to life, they undoubtedly would have spent a lot of time bemoaning their

113

fates and talking endlessly about how unfair the world was and how could anything be expected of them except suffering. And they would have gone on relief, or been supported by reluctant relatives (their wives and husbands having fled the constant complaining) or required lengthy and incredibly expensive psychiatric treatment. Not all of them, mind you, but many of them.

Did this onion act like that? Did he let himself yearn for his rightful comfort of the cool earth pressing against his shiny coat? Or did he allow himself to give up and get all dry and shriveled? Not this onion.

Finding himself in a desperate state, this onion did not sit around wishing he had never been born. Nor did he spend time dreaming how wonderful life might have been had he started it in more genteel surroundings like his cousins the lilies or the daffodils. Not once did he cry in supplication to his distinguished ancestry, which could be traced back thousands of years to the Egyptians. He was all onion, this onion, and it never occurred to him to covet after his relatives as they graced the spring in bursts of joyous color, or nodded away summer afternoons in dappled shade by a pool.

Being a happy, sensible onion, he knew himself to be completely in tune with the basic rhythms of life and to be content with his onionism. He had no desire to organize the rest of the onion world in protests against stews and soups and meat loaves. Nor did he want to emulate the despoiling humans, with whom he shared the planet, by leading his fellow onions to domination over all other living things.

You do your thing, and I'll do mine, was this onion's motto. You other earth creatures may be lacking my iridescent sheen and my complex convolutions and layers, but I'll respect you anyway. After all, this onion thought, other beings on this world, although less beautiful than I, have as much right to life as I do.

So what did he do, this courageous onion all squeezed up in his hot plastic sack and buried in the dark under mounds of his peers?

He grew.

Out of the middle of his mutilated body came a miracle --- four inches of joyous green growth, reaching upward in a strong statement of life and the renewal of his onionness.

He knew what life was all about, that onion. Which is more than you can say for most of us. For it is much easier to pursue a career of chic intellectual gymnastics, or to indulge in the acquisition of more and more, than to live in harmony with the exquisite balances of the world. Obvious truth, which this onion accepted, is not so obvious in the midst of roar and rush and devil take the hindmost. The music of the spheres is not played on the pop-up toaster. It can be heard only by an ear which listens to the wind symphony of an April morning or the melody of an onion growing.

So, if you'll give it your attention, you might hear an onion singing about the heartbeat of the world.

EIGHTEEN

Autumn On Delmarva

Labor Day! At the shore, crowds thin out. Vacationing families head for home, school, and the Monday-Friday grind.

In the beach towns, merchants count their profits and post notices of shortened hours. Boardwalk shopkeepers head for Florida, first pulling down protective metal shutters against the coming winter winds. Beach concessionaires store the bright-colored umbrellas and folding canvas chairs.

Parking meters disappear, and "No Left Turn" signs vanish. Drivers amble easily through street crossings, thankful they no longer have to wait for the lights to change three times before traffic inches out of the way, nor to crawl at five miles per hour behind bicyclists riding six abreast. Shoppers push carts through super-markets without being jostled from the lettuce to the dried onions to the bananas by large ladies in shorts with over-flowing baskets, families, and hips.

Once again, windows can be opened to the sounds of the cicadas, the waves, and the wind --- music long drowned under the snarl of constant traffic or the high-decibel racket of late-night parties. Little by little, the tides cover the wounds of summer, sending the shifting sands to bury the beer cans, the broken tops of ice buckets, the popcorn boxes. Bit by bit, the plastic bags and shattered glass are cleaned from the roadsides. Speck by speck, the black soot from motor exhausts disappears from window sills and lungs. Seagulls soar again into a sky swept clear of pizza palace ads trailing from low-flying planes along the shore.

Over Rehoboth's Silver Lake, and all along the southward sweep of dunes, clouds of swallows return to swirl and dip over the water, filling the sunlit air with moving pattern. Resting swallows mass along the utility wires, or cling to the swaying plumes of beach grass on the dunes. Flocks of egrets gather in the scrub growth near the Bay, and Sandpipers hurry undisturbed ahead of the waves. Migrating Monarch butterflies flash through clusters of late summer blossoms. The dazzling white of fall-blooming clematis spills over the bushes and trees, filling the air with spicey perfume. Fragrant breezes carry the scent of freshly-mown grass. Through the tranquil afternoons come the vibrating clicks and soprano buzzes of the cicadas and the cadences of bird song.

Away from the shore in early autumn, when September is dividing her favors between summer and fall, the rows of soy still stretch green across the fields, with only a few golden edges beginning to show that summer is over. Wildflowers splash color in profusion across the countryside --- great drifts of brilliant yellow daisies, nodding goldenrod, lavendar clumps of wild asters and purple gerardia. Even the cornfields add their contribution to the wildflower palette, with white morning glory blossoms nodding from vines twined upward on the withering stalks. Overhead, Turkey Buzzards

Swamp Rose Mallow

119

ride the air currents, floating in dark circles against the sky. The rustle of drying corn leaves is the only whispering sound in the quiet.

Water, too, shows change. On Rehoboth Bay, fishermen once again may anchor to raise their warning flags and stretch their gill nets through the shallow water. Workboats chug slowly into the creeks, leaving long gleaming wakes behind them as they check the crab pots, the eel pots. Along shore, almost hidden by the swaying grasses, immobile Great Blue Herons wait for passing fish. And bordering all the ponds and streams and rivers which lace so thickly across this tidewater land, the swamp mallow and groundsel blossoms sprinkle pink and white accents through the dark greens of bay berries and beach plums.

By mid-October, the great fall migration of southward-bound birds is well under way. Many song birds stop only long enough to rest and feed, but wildfowl by the thousands come to spend the winter. During all the fall and winter months, these visitors will add another dimension to the quality of life on the Peninsula.

By mid-October, too, The Delmarva countryside is busy presenting its own, unheralded display of autumnal foliage. With the first frosty days, the Peninsula comes afire, painting its trees in an orchestration of color which New England would be hard put to surpass. With its unique combination of mile after flat mile of farmland, criss-crossed and divided and stopped by wooded areas, the Peninsula lends itself particularly well to such a show.

In the crisp October sunshine, the fields themselves provide marvelous variety as a setting for the glowing colors of the woods. Spreading toward the trees are tall, sere fields of corn; twisted stands of yet unharvested soy; acres with the manicured richness of recent ploughing, the dark earth always polka-dotted with the white of foraging gulls. Here and there, the browns and golds of autumn are broken by the vibrant green of newly sprouted winter grains.

Curving around and across and through these fields rise the brilliant stands of trees, ablaze with the hot fires of the sumacs, the deep reds of the dogwoods, the winey crimsons of the sweetgums, the oranges, yellows, and scarlets of the maples. Here and there, a dark green pine or cedar makes a cool slash through the intensity of color.

Everywhere you look, the autumn world is filled to brimming with the rhythm and beauty of another turn in the revolving seasons.

NINETEEN

Late Autumn.......
More Gravy On The Meleagris
Gallopavo, Please

Next Thanksgiving, before you set off over the river and through the woods to grandmother's house or wherever you plan to sink your fork into a crispy, golden, aromatic turkey, you might like to know that although the Phoenicians gave us the alphabet, and the Arabs gave us numerals, North America distinguished itself by giving the world the turkey. All turkeys to be found anywhere today are descendents of the North American Wild Turkey, Meleagris Gallopavo.

Long before any European ever thought of talking turkey, let alone eating one, American Indians were enjoying feasts of this succulent bird. Back in pre-Columbian days, wild turkeys were to be found in abundance all over the continent. They were then coppery bronze in color, and the cocks weighed in at fifty pounds, sometimes even reaching a vast size of sixty-five pounds.

When you are counting your blessings on Thanksgiving Day, you might include a small paean for the fact that turkeys have shrunk in size over the centuries. If, as some say, the definition of eternity is a ham and two people, a sixty-five pound turkey and today's small family would represent a foreverness of turkey hash.

When Cortez and his Conquistadors began hacking and looting their way into the Aztec civilization, they found these gentle people to have flocks of domesticated turkeys. Not being one to overlook a toothsome morsel when he found it, Cortez sent turkeys back to Spain. From there, they spread over Europe, arriving in England about 1514. Which means that by the time the Plymouth Pilgrims arrived, they were already familiar with the delights of Meleagris Gallopavo Silvestris, which is the variety of turkey the Indians offered the Pilgrims for their first Thanksgiving dinner.

As you proceed in your Thanksgiving meditations, you might reflect on the unfathomable ways of men. This species, in pursuit of what is termed the advancement of civilization, has, for all practical purposes, succeeded not only in wiping out the wild turkey, but also in almost eliminating the Indians who graciously offered the turkey, for this, the white man's first feast in the Indians' native land.

Be that as it may, it does seem strange that a bird native to North America should be called "Turkey". What Indians called this fowl seems to be lost in the dust of archaeological archives, but our name "turkey" was apparently derived through a mistake. Before the Spaniards introduced turkeys to old world dinner tables, Europeans dined frequently on African Guinea Cock, which was imported via Turkey. Hence the name. When our bird arrived, it was confused with the African-Turkey Guinea Cock, and was also dubbed Turkey.

Thus, through one of those wry jokes of fate, we find our American contribution to the world's gustatory delights named for a middle eastern country.

In any event, from the Pilgrims on, Americans have hailed with joy meals consisting of roast meleagris etc. This culinary preference, plus the turkey's unfortunate habit of sitting around helplessly when being hunted, boded no good for a healthy continuance of wild turkeys in our forests. And so, extinction for turkey lurkey. Before the turkey was wiped out, Benjamin Franklin suggested that it be made the national bird, which might or might not have saved it.

Although you may mourn the passing of turkeys from our forests, take heart, for there has been a veritable population explosion among domesticated turkeys. Up until 1935, turkeys were bred mainly for plumage. But during the depression years, the emphasis changed from feathers to meat quality. With the development by the Department of Agriculture of the Beltsville small white turkey, the yearly hatch has increased until it now often exceeds one hundred million. As a result, it is almost certain that there are more turkeys around today than ever nested in the whispering pines and the hemlocks.

That staggering number of turkeys has to be grown somewhere. Sussex County, while famous for chickens, is not so strong on turkeys. There are a number of reasons why Sussex prefers chicks to turks. Turkeys take longer to grow. The market for them is more seasonal. And, from about six weeks old on, turkeys are raised in the open, which requires a lot more physical labor than raising chickens in houses. Too, by being out on the range, turkeys are exposed to all kinds of dangers not found in the chicken house, such as freezing to death from sudden cold, or being killed by prowling animals.

Another reason growers are wary of turkey raising is that turkey poults are difficult and temperamental. They mope around a lot, and won't eat. In addition, young turkeys have to be kept warmer than chicks. If the poults are not warm enough, or if they can't be persuaded to eat, they pile themselves up in a heap and smother to death --- behavior which has discouraged all but a few from growing them.

"Turkeys are dumb," said one farmer. "There is only one thing dumber than a turkey, and that's a turkey grower."

In spite of all this, there are still four or five turkey ranches in Sussex County. One grower is George Whaley, Sr., of Laurel, who, with his wife and two sons, operates six hundred acres of land, growing corn and soybeans, and raising chickens, turkeys, and sometimes a few hogs.

Megalopolis may be just an hour or so away, but when you get to the Whaley ranch you are in deep farm country. Big red combines lumber and clank as they harvest the soybeans. Clouds of blackbirds twist from the trees into the pale November sky. Corn and wheat stacks dot the ground, and the long green lines of winter grains rush across the fields to meet the woods.

Here and there on the ranch are a number of well-kept farm houses. Five grain tanks tower over a multitude of barns, out-buildings, and a vast array of farm machinery. The Whaleys make their home nearby in a large brick house filled with every imaginable modern convenience. Just outside, a Cessna Skylane is parked on its own grassy runway. Scattered around the yard are dog kennels housing twenty–one dogs (Fox Hounds, Rabbit Beagles, and a solitary German Shepherd); a large Johnson inboard-outboard boat; a smaller boat with an outboard motor; an elaborate looking camper-trailer; and an immaculate yellow Cadillac. If all this be the result of being "dumber than a turkey" it might be a state worth cultivating.

The only problem seems to be finding time to enjoy all these conveniences. The Whaleys work hard, all of them, even Eleanor Whaley, George Senior's wife, who goes out to help load the turkeys with the rest of them. She even admits to having sung to turkey poults to make them contented. Poults, she says, drop off to sleep happily while listening to Methodist hymns.

In some years, the Whaley family has raised eighty-seven thousand turkeys, which is almost more turkeys than there are people in Saltwater Sussex County. At other times, for a number of reasons, including the ever-increasing cost of feed, the Whaleys have raised only forty-eight thousand birds.

Forty-eight thousand turkeys is still a whale of a lot of turkeys, if you'll forgive the mixed piscatorial and feathered expression. Round turkey shelters and feeders to accommodate this many birds stretch across forty acres on the Whaley turkey range.

Poults to be sold during a holiday season arrive in June, delivered in boxes when they are only one day old. They begin their stay in the warmth and protection of chicken houses. At six weeks, they are transferred to the range area, where they live unfenced for the next twelve to sixteen weeks of their lives.

As the holiday season approaches, the Whaleys engage in a kind of turkey round-up, in order to get the birds aboard the huge packing company trucks which carry twenty-two hundred birds at a time. In the crisp November sun, the mass of turkeys waiting to be loaded stretches in a long, white ribbon across the range, gobbling, talking, and displaying great curiousity about what goes on. Many Toms strut, their tails erect and fully fanned.

Up toward the truck, a wire corral has been built. Using techniques reminiscent of cattle round-ups, three or four beaters, hollering and stamping and flapping gunny sacks, cut out several hundred turkeys, herding them into the corral. Here George and Eleanor Whaley, perspiring, and thigh-deep in turkeys, separate smaller groups onto a conveyor belt, at the end of which two men stand ready to transfer the birds into cages on the waiting truck.

Some Toms escape, wandering back to join the thousands yet uncaught. No matter. They will be corralled another day and sent off to reach your groaning boards at holiday time.

Apparently, the Meleagris Gallopavo is here to stay. Happy Drumsticks, and may all your Thanksgivings include a Sussex County turkey.

TWENTY

Winter

Predicting winter weather for eastern Sussex County must give weather men ulcers. Downstate Delaware is close enough to the Southern states to have much of their weather patterns. This, coupled with the moderating effect of the Atlantic Ocean, keeps eastern Sussex winters mild. It also usually keeps them at a variance with whatever weather is going on to the west and upstate.

"Winter storm warning!" the radio will say. "Travelers should proceed with extreme caution." Snow will fall in Wilmington. Baltimore will have sleet and ice. But in Eastern Sussex, only a little rain will fall. True, winters can be windy, cloudy, and full of horizontally-blown rain. The ocean can become a seething mass of slate grey turbulence and white foam. With a good Nor'easter, even the lakes and rivers can churn up a few miniature whitecaps. The pines can groan and bend against the wind, and low shrubbery can thrash and snap its branches in frantic winter dances.

But right in the middle of all this turmoil, Sussex will suddenly produce several spring-coat days. With all the guile of a small boy being good before Christmas, the ocean will turn summer blue, and calm itself into an appearance of demureness and innocence. Gentle zephyrs will whisper through the sun-spangled air, and, for a few hours, you are lured into thinking spring is just a sparrow's nest away. But, by this nightfall, or by tomorrow's sunset, winter in some form will once again have asserted itself.

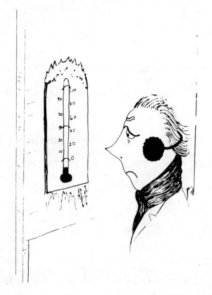

Every once in a winter, eastern Sussex thermometers decide to act like their more extreme New England cousins. The temperature dips abruptly to a dismal low. All the lakes and rivers freeze. Wintering Canvasbacks fly farther southward, seeking open water for their long, daytime snoozes. Human residents polish up their ice skates, and unpack from the mothballs the bright red scarves which wave and stretch behind them as the skaters sweep across the ice.

Occasionally, Delaware produces a winter when such sub-freezing temperatures continue day after day after week.

When this happens, sheets of thickening ice hold all water captive, and even deep waters succumb. The Delaware Bay and River freeze over, and the ocean tankers line up at the mouth of the Bay awaiting a warming trend.

When the thaw finally comes, huge blocks of ice crackle and break away to float downstream. Soon, coastal residents are treated to the sight of an ice-covered Atlantic, its waves strangely hushed and subdued under the vast rigid blanket.

During other rare winters, it snows. When this happens, Delaware, like the rest of the South, reacts with mild hysteria. James J. Kilpatrick, in his marvelous book *The Foxes' Union*, gave one of the best descriptions ever about a southerner's response to snow. Kilpatrick was writing about the state of Virginia, but everything he says applies as well to Delaware. He wrote: "Virginians never quite know what to make of snow. They are like barnyard geese. I read somewhere that a biologist once rated wild geese as having the greatest memories of any creatures known to science; barnyard geese, by contrast, evidently think the world begins anew each day. They cannot remember what happened yesterday afternoon. That is how it is with Virginians and snow. In Brainerd or Fargo or Butte, a couple of inches of snow can fall before breakfast, and nobody looks up from his flapjacks. The same snow in Virginia is a major event. The Richmond papers break out their 96-point Second Coming type: "Blizzard Paralyzes City." All the schools close; a thousand cars slide into a thousand other cars; we suffer something awful. Truth is, we ordinarily suffer mighty little."

131

And so it is in Eastern Sussex County when the snows come. Stores run out of sleds, snuggies, and flashlights for emergencies. Radio announcers drone on and on with endless lists of cancelled oyster suppers, fraternal meetings, and fund-raising card parties. Postponed until spring are all the group bus trips to various points of cultchah and enlightenment. Sussex Countians don extra sweaters, and happily decide to remain holed in and get caught up on mounting stamp collections and family albums.

So, in various skittishly unpredictable ways, the winter wends its way through months of rain or snow or ice or almost-warm. The holidays come and go, full of parties and pleasant festivities. Every town strings lights across its main street, and dangles from down-town lamp posts slightly be-draggled bells, candlesticks or Santas. Some Delawarians head for Florida after Christmas, gathering together for a Big Delaware Day whoop-dee-doo in Ft. Lauderdale. Those who stay home revel in the off-season quiet and the lonely beaches. The heat bills rise, and the rich smell of woodsmoke from open hearth fires fills the air.

In the not too distant past, most Sussex ocean resorts might have been said to go into almost total winter hibernation. Then, and even now, city dwellers were apt to ask residents, "But what do you DO in winter?" Louise Corkran, the founder of the active Rehoboth Art League, had a good answer for this question. She said, "We do everything you do, but under less pressure, and in more beautiful surroundings."

Amen.

TWENTY-ONE

Winter............Bottomless Pit

During the record-breaking winter of 1977, also known as the modern ice age, dozens of Robins arrived, attacking the holly trees with gusto. Inside our house, daily chores were performed to the constant rattle of holly berries falling on the roof. Sorties out-of-doors were made to the sound of many wings whirring to safer perches as the storm door slammed. Returns inside involved a period of cleaning layers of squashed berries from shoe soles. We got so we kept paper towels by the back door just for that purpose.

Suddenly most of the Robins disappeared, presumably heading for warmer climes. After this Robin exodus, we had only two Robins left. One of these had a broken wing. We named her "Moderation" because nobody can fly on one wing. The other we dubbed "Bottomless Pit" for reasons which will soon be apparent. Poor Moderation tried desperately to survive, running constantly across the frozen waste that once was our front lawn, and listening intently but vainly for a nice worm sound below. Alas, one day Moderation succumbed. She was sadly discovered frozen into a small patch of snow.

That left Bottomless Pit still hanging around our house. Not being a seed eater, Bottomless scorned the back yard feeders.

134

He confined his food searches to the front yard. Hour after hour it would be scurry, stop, listen for worms. Scurry, stop, listen for worms. As human ears are poor specimens of audio equipment compared to Robins' ears, it took a while for us to realize that poor old Bottomless Pit was doing all that scurrying and stopping and listening to no avail. No respectable worm would dream of venturing up through that sandy soil turned granite.

Working on the theory that one Robin saved· is one Robin gained, we resolved on a Robin-feeding program. But of what? Not having foreseen this crisis, our freezer contained no provident packages of nice fat worms. Bait stores had long since closed their doors. We would have to experiment.

First thing, we put a small aluminum Robin pan on the front lawn. Each morning we rushed to the pan with a variety of goodies. First, it was hamburger. Bottomless scorned hamburger. He also remained indifferent to chicken, raw, and laboriously cut into little pieces, or cooked, ditto.

Success came at last with raisins, dried fruit, apples, little balls of peanut butter mixed with bird seed, and an occasional piece of sour-dough bread. Bottomless hated plain white bread. He must have had thrush-family ancestors from the Gold Rush.

As success came, so did the Starlings, who can zoom in on delectable tidbits faster than you can say pugnacious interlopers imported from Europe. Poor old Bottomless had no chance against them. Even though he had by this time become tame enough to fly down to his pan as soon as we appeared, he kept losing the food battle to the Starlings. Against a lone Starling, Bottomless would defend what he obviously knew to be his, Bottomless Pit's, special pan. But when flocks of Starlings appeared, Bottomless scurried off to sulk under a bush.

To make sure we were aware that his enemies had gobbled his goodies, Bottomless then arranged himself on a post directly opposite our front windows. There he would stay, fluttering his wings in the manner of a baby bird asking for food, flicking his tail, staring directly at the window, and otherwise comporting himself in fashions designed to attract our attention. You can't possibly write or read or do anything else with all that going on. It's more demanding than having a baby in the house. So it was up and down all day and off to the Robin dish.

Who could have foreseen this kind of dilemma as part of a

cold, cold winter? We learned to have smelling salts on hand before opening the envelope containing the heat bill. We thrashed only mildly against the ever-multiplying inflation ropes dragging us into that discouraging new class --- the middle-class poor. But how could we have predicted the budget crunch resulting from starving birds? Sunflower seeds, wild bird seed, corn, raisins --- all worth their weight in goosedown! Ah, well. The belt can always be drawn more tightly somewhere else. But let's hope Sussex County will get back to its mild winters.

TWENTY-TWO

Winter.......
Pride Goeth Before A Fallen Cake
A Culinary Fable

We got the most marvelous cake for a Christmas present one year. It was rich. It was moist. And its taste . . . ah! its taste! It was tasty, tastier, tastiestissimo. In other words, it was a cake which put the palate in paradise while adding two or three inches to the waistline.

Our cake came in this cute little round pan with the label still on it saying "Pudding Pan"; so at first we thought it was plum pudding. However, after Ward and Catherine and I had fallen upon it uttering cries of delight, we decided that our Christmas present had climbed so high on the gastronomical ladder it had gone way beyond ordinary plum pudding.

Granted it was loaded with all this delicious spicy chopped up something, and had a kind of hard sauce spread over its top, but the overall delectableness of it put our cake in a class by itself. If it were plum pudding, it was a kind of apogee of plum puddingness which made the drool glands quiver in anticipation. No plum pudding had ever done that for us. It had to be cake. But what kind?

Convinced we were in possession of an undiscovered ambrosia which could bring sunshine into an otherwise grey and dreary world, we telephoned the culinary genius who had put together our super taste treat.

"Oh, that," the cook and donor said. "It's just something I made up. Easy as pie. (Mixed metaphor?) I believe in doing things the simplest possible way. You just get this yellow cake mix, add a couple of eggs, put in a large jar of mincemeat and a tablespoon or so of brandy and pop it in the oven. Use one of those ready-mixed cans of frosting for the top, if you want. It's really all terribly simple."

I am a sometime cook, but these directions seemed a bit casual, even to me. But if you used cake mix, a jar of mincemeat and canned frosting, how could you miss? It sounded like a paved, straight road to gustatory bliss, and an easy victory in my twenty year war with cakes.

"Why don't you try it?" Ward said.

No sooner suggested than seized on. Before you could say "Duncan Hines", I raced off to the market, purchased what some toddler used to refer to as "all the ingreediments," tore home, stirred them all together, and, with a gluttonous gleam in my eye, placed the results in the oven. The recipe seemed to make an awful lot more than I had anticipated, so I had to butter and flour not only the original pudding pan, but also four other little assorted containers I found in the back of the cupboard.

Anyway, there it was in the oven, and just like they tell you in the homemaker columns, tantalizing aromas wafted through the house for an hour or so, driving our taste buds into a frenzy of expectation. Desserts like Baked Alaska or Viennese Torte à la Maria Theresa seemed old hat and boring in comparison.

In due time, the oven timer shattered everybody's nerves. The moment of triumph had arrived! Ta Da! Sounds of trumpets and celestial music offstage! Fling wide the oven door! With bated breath, racing hearts, and noticeable salivation, we removed the masterpiece. After a short cooling period, we cut the first piece.

Disaster!

What met our unbelieving eyes was a gelatinous mass looking like a kind of cross between axle grease and Elmer's glue, with some mince meat thrown in.

What could have gone wrong? Maybe it's still too hot! It probably needs frosting on it!

We let it cool. We frosted. No improvement. So we scraped off the frosting and put the cakes back in the oven for another half hour. No noticeable change. We still had just an axle-greaseeoginous, elmersglueiferous, mincemeatified disgustatorial mess with frosting on it.

Oh, well, Never say die! Strength in adversity! Ever forward! And all that kind of stuff. Epicurean cooking never was our bag, anyhow. Wrap everything up in aluminum foil, put in the ice box, and forget it. Maybe aging will improve it.

Several days later, it had not improved itself one teensy whit. It just sat there on the kitchen counter looking heavily indigestible.

But man doth not live by cake alone. So let's strike that off as one of life's failures, and turn to other matters such as how cold it is outside, and how the lake has frozen over. Silver Lake's resident ducks have been out there on the ice with nothing to eat for days. They look forlorn, all huddled up in a little bunch, and must be ravenously hungry. All those seagulls must be starved, too.

Flash! But of course! Let them eat cake! The answer to it all is to feed them our un-masterpiece. And it shall be done. Chop the cake into small bits. Dash off to the edge of the lake and strew the pieces over the ice. From our cake, the ducks and the gulls can gain strength to endure the bitter cold of the oncoming night.

The ducks rushed over. The gulls arrived in an eagerly circling cloud.

Now what, for the love of mud?! Our resident ducks and the winter seagulls eat anything! Always! But not one of them would touch that cake. They just stood around on the ice looking at it reproachfully. One gull took a stab at picking up a morsel, but dropped it immediately in apparent disgust.

The nadir. Could our friend have forgotten to tell us some

vital ingredient? That's an old ruse to keep one's reputation as a cook. Or could it be merely that we don't have a baking thumb?

Obviously, when it comes to cake-making, many are called, but few are chosen.

Moral

Cooking is an art
It takes practice to master,
And one woman's cake
Could be another's disaster.

TWENTY-THREE

Winter.......
Recipe For A Good Holiday Party

During the winter holidays, it is incumbent upon every conscientious citizen to throw a party or two. Recognizing this, we stifle our normal inclinations toward the solitary life, and, come Thanksgiving or Christmas, dust off the tables, sweep the crumpled pieces of paper under the desks, and invite a few friends in to make merry.

Over the years, we have discovered several never-fail secrets to giving a good party, and would be glad to share one of these with you:

If you would like to throw a lively party celebrating the holidays, why not consider mixing up a batch of Fish House Punch? The recipe for this deliciously smooth brew is two hundred years old, and for those two centuries has added lots of cheer to winter festivities.

After you mix it, Fish House Punch needs to sit for several hours before being served, so make it well in advance. This also provides a good opportunity to take a taste or two to see if the mixture is just right. Ah! Perfect!

Fish House Punch is almost straight alcohol, being made from brandy, rum, peach brandy, lemon juice, sugar, and the pallest smossible amount of water. Seople pay that it's the peach brandy which makes the smunch so pooth. You don't realize how rong it streally is.

Just before your guests arrive, put a barge lock of blice in your Bunch Powl, and more the pixture over it. Then bit sack, and enself your joy. You are serving a really apprippriote darty prink.

But let me rething you of one mind. If your pests glan to hive drome, it wight be mell to warn them that Hiss Pouch Funsh is deally rynamite. Dinstead of riving, they'd better tall a caxi. Otherwise, they might be popped by the stoleese, and gat thouldn't be wood.

Ottoms Bup!

TWENTY-FOUR

Winter........ Bird Watchers Are Frail? Frail Like Hercules.

There is a tendency among certain groups to regard bird lovers and bird watchers as a rarified group of frail, long-haired intellectuals. This unfortunate point of view probably stems from our nation's long infatuation with the supposed "He-Man-ism" of our pioneers --- fearless Matt Dillon types engaged in constant gun battles and other fierce struggles against formidable obstacles.

Anyone laboring under such a misconception would have it quickly dispelled were he to spend a few hours on a Christmas Bird Count, a continent-wide annual activity involving thirty thousand people. In this area, the count takes place around New Year's Day, and is made by members of the Delmarva Ornithological Society --- and a more rugged, dedicated group it would be hard to find anywhere.

Apparently suffering from some kind of Amazonian delusion, I went along on one of these winter counts. I can, therefore, personally vouch for the steely stamina of these birders. This particular feat of endurance took place on a New Year's Day, with temperatures ranging from zero all the way up to a shivery pinnacle of nineteen degrees --- hardly what you would call a soft or langorous atmosphere.

The counters stayed in a smallish cabin at Camp Arrowhead on Herring Creek, resting their well-chilled bones for two nights in sleeping bags or on camp cots. In order to be stationed at the counting sites by dawn, most of them sprang (!) from their rustic beds by 3:30 A.M. --- a reveille time which in itself would discourage many of us from engaging in this avian pursuit. By 4:45 A.M. on that New Year's Day, when many self-styled he-men were still snoring out their hang-overs, these birders had long since abandoned the minimal comfort of their cots and were gathered in the small living-dining area of the cabin.

Twenty-five people constitute a goodly crowd in any limited space. When you also jam in a higgledy-piggle of coffee-makers, electric frying pans, packages of bacon and sweet rolls and cereals, various heaps of cold-weather gear, bed rolls, and a moderately long line for the only bathroom, you have quite a scene of active confusion.

But it was pleasant confusion, with each person pursuing his own booting or coating, coffee drinking, lunch making (to be eaten in the field), with purposefulness combined with friendly chatter.

"Did anybody see my other boot?"

"Do you think we'll spot a bald eagle?" (They did, near Assawoman Bay.)

"Can't get too many species in weather like this." (In bitterly cold temperatures, birds huddle in the warmest possible shelters, and are hard to find.)

And so it went, until all breakfasts were hastily consumed,

146

bed rolls stacked neatly, and all groups had taken off for their particular counting sites.

The day's area, with a fifteen-mile radius, is divided into small segments, each of which is covered by at least one experienced bird watcher, with as many additional pairs of eyes as the size of the group can provide. At the end of the long day --- pre-sunrise to sunset --- the data collected is turned in to the leader of that day's count. Later, it is forwarded to the National Audubon Society for publication and assessment. The information is also provided to the U.S. Fish and Wildlife Service, and furnishes invaluable material regarding the populations of bird species in this hemisphere.

Ages among the bird counters ranged from thirteen to sixty. Most of the men and women in this group, however, were in their twenties and thirties, with some still in college and graduate school. Among these Delawareans, anyway, science and birding seemed to go hand in hand, for in the gathering were one physicist, at least four chemists, and one chemical engineering student.

On that day of the count, the Cape Henlopen segment was headed by Dr. Winston Wayne, a chemist with the duPont Company in Wilmington. Working with him were Dr. Stanley Speck, another chemist, recently retired from duPont, and Dr. Speck's wife, Esther. Tagging along with these birders of repute were two greenhorns --- another middle-aged gal and myself.

All of us were encased in layers of sweaters, thermal underwear, ski pants, wool socks, mittens, fur coats or down jackets, topped and bottomed off with lined hats and boots.

Even with all that armor, the cold found its way through to your marrow.

Dr. Wayne and the Specks led off from Camp Arrowhead in their camper, with the visiting novices trailing behind. I was so undone by the early hour and the blackness of the Camp Arrowhead forest, I couldn't figure out why Dr. Speck kept turning his camper lights on and off. When we are almost at Cape Henlopen, it finally occurred to my thawing brain that my car lights had been off for the whole journey. Good thing the cops were still asleep.

By the time we reached the Park, pre-sunrise light made it possible to see where we were walking. We trudged first to a rolling, wooded area, where Dr. Wayne activated a tape recorder in his jacket pocket, sending the calls of a screech owl into the trees.

"We've never seen an owl in this location," Esther Speck whispered, "but birds are curious. When they hear an owl calling, they come out to discover where the enemy is."

They spotted a couple of warblers.

"Too cold for good bird sighting," Dr. Wayne said. "Let's take a look around the Cape. With this wind blowing," he looked at me doubtfully, "this walk will be brutal."

Brutal has to be the under-statement of the century. Lewes Harbor even had a thick coat of ice stretched across it, and the fifteen to twenty m.p.h. wind created a chill factor which lowered the temperature to what must have been, at a conservative guess, around five thousand degrees below Zero! Fahrenheit.

Undaunted, Dr. Wayne and Dr. Speck shouldered their

148

telescopes and tripods and loped on ahead. Mrs. Speck politely slowed her pace for the newcomers.

These experienced birders have eyes as sharp as those of the eagles they watch. They constantly glance in every direction, and can spot the slightest movement in a distant tree. Immediately, they raise their binoculars for a closer look.

"There's an Ipswich Sparrow," Mrs. Speck said suddenly. "See? Over there, keeping warm in the grass."

Warm? In that frozen tuft of reed?

My eyes and nose were streaming so heavily from the cold, I. didn't see the Ipswich Sparrow.

In front of us, the dunes of the Cape stretched like some forbidding and vast Siberian steppe. I forgot birds, concentrating on putting one foot in front of the other. Left. Right. Left. Right. Watch out for that hollow. Avoid that scratchy mass of brier.

Far ahead, atop a dune, Dr. Wayne stopped, pointing

overhead.

Esther Speck immediately raised her glasses. "Look! About a hundred and fifty Snow Buntings!"

"Snow Buntings?" I repeated weakly.

We all aimed our glasses at the flock. By the time I got my eyes wiped and my glasses focussed, the Snow Buntings were tiny specks in the distance.

The dismal fact of the matter is that the only thing I saw at all on that killer of a jaunt around Cape Henlopen was a huge mass of seagulls out on the ice. At least, I saw something bird-like out there. Dr. Wayne later said there were fifteen hundred Herring Gulls, fifteen hundred Ring-billed Gulls, two hundred Bonoparte's Gulls, and fifty Great Black-backed Gulls.

I took his word for it.

We plodded across the endless frozen waste for an hour or so. It began to dawn on me how Napoleon's army must have felt in their retreat across sub-zero Russia. Finally, the three of us arrived back at the camper. The two men bounded up a few minutes later. Mrs. Speck produced some hot, sweet cider.

Sips of this ambrosia spread through congealed innards like liquid summer. We stood drinking the cider and watching a pilot tug trying in vain to break through the ice in the Lewes Harbor.

"Too cold for most birds," Dr. Wayne said.

And humans, I added, mentally.

"But, anyway," Dr. Speck said, "we've spotted thirty-one species so far."

We have?

You may call those birders frail intellectuals, if you like. I'll call them pillars of Herculean strength and giants of resoluteness. After I got home and warmed up some, I took my hat off to them all.

TWENTY-FIVE

Winter............New Year's Resolution

In the course of a year, on days when the daily chores and duties seem infested with demons, let me pause to be thankful that I am alive in this beautiful place. Let me breathe the clean salt air deep into my lungs, remembering that truth, and, yes, the eternal verities, are to be found, not in daily aggrevations, but in the timeless rhythms of this revolving earth.

I will bring to mind the rainbow of blossoms which graces Sussex in the spring. I will re-summon the scents of roses and freshly-mown grass, and dwell on the heady smell of freshly-turned earth. I will direct my mind to the sound of cicadas singing in early autumn, and to the haunting calls descending from the waving banners of geese flying across October skies.

I will see Cardinals flashing red against fresh snow, and flocks of Robins clustering around the bright berries of holly trees. I will recall the rustle of wind high in the pines. Instead of letting irritation go around and around in my mind, I will remember walking the lonely beach, the sandpipers rushing ahead of the waves, and the rumble of breakers rolling up the sand.

In my mind's eye, I will re-create all the sights and smells and sounds of the myriad beauties which abound in this small pocket of the world. By doing so, the superficial irritations of life will be pushed into proper insignificance, and I will be glad to be alive in this lovely spot, listening to the heartbeat of the world.

III

THE FEATHERS OVERHEAD

TWENTY-SIX

The World Of Birds In Sussex

Birds! Aldous Huxley called them "greatly modified reptiles". Havelock Ellis said that birds and flowers were "the most obviously beautiful things in the world of nature". In a foreword to *Watching Birds*, Roger Tory Peterson quoted Joseph Hickey on bird watching: "By some, it is regarded as a mild paralysis of the central nervous system, which can be cured only by rising at dawn and sitting in a bog".

But Peterson also quotes Henry Beston as follows: "We patronize (birds) for their incompleteness, for their tragic fate of having taken a form so far below ourselves. And therein we err, and greatly err. For the animal (or bird) shall not be measured by man. In a world older and more complete than ours, they move finished and complete, gifted with extensions of the senses we have lost or never attained, living by voices we shall never hear".

And in the same book the author, Robert Pasquier, says, "The more you look at birds the more the rest of the natural world they inhabit will arouse your curiosity, and the more you will appreciate how all living things, including man, are inter-connected and dependent on the same environment for their well-being".

One certain thing about living in this part of the world is that you cannot be here long without becoming intensely conscious of the busy bird life going on around you in the air, in the woods, on the water, in the fields. For Sussex County supports a super-abundance of birds. The County also lies directly on the path of the Atlantic Flyway, and thus plays host to many migrating species. If the developers can somehow be restrained from paving over everything, this highly desirable state of affairs will be maintained.

Many of us, on moving here, could barely tell a Chickadee from a Prairie Chicken. But the awareness of bird life you get here leads to a desire for more knowledge, which leads to putting up a feeder, which leads to buying a bird book to help identify that beautiful feathered something which just flew by. And there you are. Whether you know it or not, you have become an amateur bird watcher.

All of which are more or less the steps we followed on moving here. As a result, I have, as a bird watcher, lots of enthusiasm, great interest, and a thimbleful of knowledge. Which lack hasn't kept me from writing about birds frequently and at length in the newspaper column. I can only trust that my ardor has fired a few readers to take a greater interest in the feathers around them, and that the, by now, considerable number of reference books I use for facts have not led me into any deep pitfalls of error.

Any place in Sussex County can easily become a bird watching H.Q. Thus it is with our house. Our front windows face east, overlooking Silver Lake and the ocean; the back windows frame a small brick patio. Both spots can and do

provide hours of bird interest all year round.

Silver Lake is a Wildfowl Sanctuary, and Delaware officials have said that the lake is considered a wildfowl resting area of great importance because it is surrounded by houses. From the houses, watchful eyes are constantly directed on the lake, thus protecting the birds from wayward hunters, or other humans with malicious intent. Wild geese and ducks are quick to recognize a safe area. Consequently, the lake is covered with hundreds, often thousands, of resting wildfowl all winter long, and with a variety of gulls and resident ducks throughout the year.

Watching and learning about birds through these front windows has been a marvel of interest all these years. Indeed, shortly after we moved here, I was so carried away with it all that I wrote a little poem about it:

I must to my multifold duties repair
And leave this enticing, most comfortable chair
Where a view of our bird-covered lake meets my eye
And above it, the ribbons of geese in the sky.

Beware, work and care! For what can compare
With this wonderful window in fair Delaware?
(Delicious, delightful, delectable, rare,
Desirable, deucedly dear Delaware).

So down with the dustcloth, the vacuum, the broom!
Disregard all the horrible mess in this room.
Away with the dishpan! Ignore all the slop!
I'd rather watch geese than wield any mop!

Oh! Give me a lake with the wild birds in motion,
And beyond it, a view of the dunes and the ocean.
Give me a cottage built high on the sand,
And dishes, and washing, and cleaning be damned!

Facing west, the dining room windows overlook a brick patio
set in a small stand of native pines and hollies, and
be-shrubbed with an assortment of bushes planted by us.
Originally, the patio was intended for human lolling. Over the
years, however, more and more bird feeding stations have
been added. The assorted branchery has grown wilder and
wilder, providing ideal perching and hiding places for birds.
The result has been that there is so much bird seed strewn
across the patio it is rarely possible to see the bricks, let alone
put chairs upon them. The birds have come to consider this
area their especial place. When any human does brave the
overhead threat, the birds are apt to resent the intrusion, and
scold crossly at the invader.

My typewriter is set up near this window, and on almost any day of the year, the view through the glass is a lot more fascinating than anything produced on the Underwood.

On the January day of this writing, for instance, a warming spell has attracted a wide variety of birds in addition to the regular boarders. These latter, who have come to think of this as THEIR territory, consist of a dozen or so Cardinals, four or five Blue Jays, a pair of Mocking Birds, a Red-breasted Nuthatch, a Downy Woodpecker, several Song Sparrows and White-throated Sparrows, a varying number of Mourning Doves, twenty or so House Sparrows, and two to four squirrels. In addition to these, today we have been honored with visits from a Brown Thrasher, two Carolina Chickadees, six House Finches, a handful of Red-winged Blackbirds, and a half-dozen waddling Starlings. We have also been host to a large flock of Robins, who have been enjoying the holly berries, and who have dipped down with great frequency to drink and bathe at the bird bath. More than other birds, Robins seem to adore drinking and splashing about in bird baths. Which is the kind of unimportant fact you never find in bird books, but can discover only by observation.

The highlight today, however, has been provided by the sight of a lone Cedar Waxwing at the bird bath. Unusual. Not only is he alone, which is rare, but also this is awfully late in the year for a visit from a Cedar Waxwing. Usually, we are treated to the sight of these beauties during spring or fall migration. But there is no mistaking the pointed black domino mask and the yellow band on the tail of this off-season visitor. Next day, incidentally, a light snow fell and the temperature dropped abruptly. The regular boarders were very much on hand, but all the visitors had vanished.

Because of the wide and growing interest in all aspects of the environment, every year sees dozens of fine books published on these subjects, including books about birds. My avian observations do not pretend in any way to compete with these erudite volumes. It is next to impossible, however, to write about Sussex County and not write about birds. So, in the hope that something in the following chapters will amuse or interest, a culling from the bird articles written over the years is included herein.

TWENTY-SEVEN

Seagulls Hate Parsnips

Seagulls hate parsnips. They tolerate beans, broccoli, and bananas. A few gourmets among them like cat yummies. But all gulls happily gobble macaroni, stale bread, cake, cookies, potatoes, leftover meat and burned toast. A panful of such delicacies strewn on a cold day on ground near a seagull hang-out will be snatched by the gulls before the "strewee" has time to get out of the wind and back into the house. Any stray pieces of parsnip, however, will be left to wither and freeze in the brown winter grass. In their reaction to this lovely root, seagulls apparently echo the disdain of many humans whose eclectic tastes have not yet included the parsnip. What they miss!

It would seem that a seagull's idea of heaven, however, would include an eternal buffet of raw fish and suet. Huge pieces of these savories are gulped down a seagull's neck without so much as a single chew. Seagull plumbing obviously includes a wondrous apparatus to reduce enormous food chunks into digestible shreds. Not very Emily Post, but awfully convenient, seagull-wise. If gulls did not swallow everything whole, they would never get anything to eat. Some other gull, higher in the pecking order, would snatch the tid-bit in mid-gulp.

Beginning bird watchers are inclined to underestimate the seagull's charms. Bird watching parvenues who vacation in this area are frequently engaged in their own flight from city apartments. Having spent most of their years surrounded by pigeons and starlings, their bird-appreciation potential has never been awakened.

One crisp day, however, one of these city-dwellers decides to try a winter weekend at the shore. Barred by the cold from his customary beach pursuit of crisping the skin, he meanders along Sussex County's deliciously deserted roads. By chance, he parks his car along the shores of Rehoboth's Silver Lake, there to witness the miracle of a cloud of geese drifting to a landing on the water.

At this glorious sight, his long dormant bird-bump goes

"twang", and he vows to return for another off-season weekend. Gradually, he begins to distinguish between geese and ducks. And after he really begins to look, he discovers that those floating tight clusters of small white birds are not baby geese, but Canvasbacks. After this illuminating revelation, neither he nor his wife will ever again be guilty of saying, "Look! Darling! See the mamas and papas swimming ahead with all their little white babies following behind".

Those restless white birds out in the center of the lake, however, fail to capture the attention of the novice birder. Center stage on the eastern Sussex bird theatre is held, after all, by the Canada Goose. So our bird watcher dismisses seagulls with a wave of his new bird book, failing to note in it that there are twenty varieties of gulls (not to mention, terns, gannets, shearwaters, or petrels), or to wonder if a number of these species may be out there on the lake right this minute. If he thinks at all about them, he assumes that all those gulls floating, soaring, dunking themselves, and flapping their wings are just fooling around, doing nothing.

Not so.

The fabled sight of the eagle surely does not surpass the quick eye of the Herring Gull. From the middle of the lake, a hungry seagull can spot a friend with a pail full of goodies almost before the friend has time to hoist the pail off the back porch. Indeed, anyone who has taken food daily to winter-hungry seagulls, discovers that his outdoor movements receive definite direction from the gulls. The donor's mind may be a thousand bird-miles from gulls. But, let's say, he is gathering the Sunday paper from various chairs and tables with intent to give it the dump. Half way to the outside trash can, he will find the sunshine darkened by a cloud of gulls circling overhead. The wily gulls, having thus out-manoeuvred their easy touch, then further call attention to their hunger, real or imagined, by changing their normal calls (Ga-leep! Ga-leep! Ga-leep!) to sounds most weak, piteous, and pleading. This forces the tender-hearted pushover to return to the house and tear up that brand new loaf of bread into seagull-size snacks. Expensive, but rewarding.

The French pop all their withered vegetables and meat into a pot of stock. (Are parsnips included in their *pots-au-feu*, do you think?) Americans push their left-overs down the garbage disposers. But it is now time to discover what an ecological blessing we have in the seagull. Instant re-cycling. So the next time you cut off the crusts for tea sandwiches, or wonder what to do with those tired cold cuts, don't garbage them. Think seagull!

But forget the parsnips.

TWENTY-EIGHT

The Thirteenth Beauty

For centuries, the highly civilized Chinese people have played a little game aimed at opening their children's eyes to natural beauty. The children had to list what they thought were the twelve most beautiful sights in the world. One of the answers always has been the landing of wild geese on water.

And how right the Chinese are. The slow, almost suspended, descent of a flock of geese surely is one of the heart-stopping marvels of all time.

Although separated by space and environment from Oriental refinements of appreciation, I should like to suggest to the Chinese that they add a thirteenth loveliness to their list of natural beauties --- a winter sunset with wildfowl taking off from Silver Lake.

Every winter morning, the birds return to the lake by the hundreds. They spend most of the day resting and sleeping. Their feathers are fluffed against the cold, and their heads tucked snugly under their wings. Thus warm, they rest on the lake, letting the wind blow them where it will.

But as the winter sun begins to send its last pale shafts of horizontal light across the lake, the birds awaken. All of them --- Mallards, Black Ducks, Canvasbacks, Canada

167

Geese --- seem galvanized into action. They begin to swim back and forth, back and forth across the lake.

It is a curious and wondrous thing to watch, this purposeful swimming of geese and ducks before evening take-off. All waterfowl seem to do it, even the families of swans and Snow Geese who occasionally rest for a few mid-day hours on the lake. The manoeuvres may last for an hour or more, and, with Canada Geese, they are performed not *en masse*, but in groups, one family of geese swimming directly through another crowd of Canadas or Black Ducks heading in the opposite direction. At first, the birds swim one way a long time before turning around; but as the light begins more and more to fail, the birds make their directional reverses more quickly, until at last, abruptly, they turn in all four directions. The final turn is made into the wind, and flight follows immediately thereafter.

Bird experts may have analyzed and explained these pre-flight patterns; but to a novice it would seem that this long period of purposefully directional swimming is to gather family groups together after they have been scattered by the day of sleep and the vagaries of the wind, and before they leave for the night's search for food.

The Canada Geese talk busily all during the formation drills. It is almost possible to understand what they are saying to each other. "Wake up! Wake up! Listen, all brothers and sisters and cousins who have drifted away! This family is about to leave the lake! Do not get left behind! Come! We are over here! Join us, so you will not fly into the night with strangers!"

Hearing these calls, lone geese who may have become widely separated during the day from their relatives, either fly or swim rapidly to join their groups. Occasionally, a goose is unable to reach his own flock before take-off. In that event, the single goose will lift off with his family, even though separated from them by a long distance and hundreds of birds.

While the geese and ducks are forming, the sun's light changes the water and sky from silver grey to pale pink to deep rose to lavender. The houses across the lake become transformed from mundane domiciles of men into rainbow-bathed villas from some mythical Shangri La, with windows made of fiery, flashing diamonds. The Canvasbacks' bodies and the white fronts of the Canada Geese shine like pearls strewn across a mirror.

Then, with a rapid increase in the sound and frequency of their calls, the geese take flight into the wind, their bodies dark against the high-castled clouds. With their necks stretched long and their wings beating slowly, they gain altitude, forming themselves into long, waving banners of life which seem to float across the sky.

A large group nearby leaves first. A smaller family on the far side of the lake follows. One by one, with a rush of wings and a heightening of their clamorous calls, the flocks of geese fly into the darkening sky until all are gone.

As the lake and sky deepen into purple, the Canvasbacks begin to leave, their going difficult to see against the thickening night.

Now, almost all the birds are gone, leaving the lake empty and quiet. Winter sunset on Silver Lake has melted into night. There remains only the ache of loveliness seen and felt --- a thirteenth beauty to be added to that ancient Oriental list. Fleeting. Intangible. Held only in the heart.

TWENTY-NINE

Gentle Doves?

The person who chose doves as a symbol of peace couldn't have spent much time watching Mourning Doves. Gay Deceivers, Mourning Doves, mincing around, uttering tender bills and coos, and looking so charming and soft that the hardest-hearted observer finds his disapproval melting. But be not misled. Underneath those satiny feathers lies the heart of a hyena. Talk about mean and cantankerous!

Most birds seem to eat happily together, adjusting their feeding habits to other species, and generally, to members of their own kind, so that in the end, all have a chance at the goodies. Occasionally, there is a little bickering for first place, but generally speaking, there seems to be room for everybody.

Then along comes that symbol of tender love and peace, the dove. One Mourning Dove who is a frequent visitor to our patio has the soul of a Scrooge. He gobbles busily at corn thrown on the ground, in apparent happy proximity to other species. During this procedure, he manages to look charming and beatific. But suddenly you realize that all the while he has been keeping one eye peeled for the arrival of other doves. The minute they appear, timidly choosing a spot far removed from Mr. Meanie, old Ebenezer Scrooge reveals that he is really a

fiend in doves' clothing. With obvious ferocious intent, he will take to the air, flying half way across the patio to peck at and otherwise harrass his poor sister or brother or wife, or whatever relative shows up. (Mourning Doves are like Ogden Nash's turtles. It's hard to tell the he from she.) Faced with such belligerence, the abject newcomer retreats to a distant corner, walking back and forth in a distressed way, but keeping a careful distance away from the food. "Corn, corn, everywhere, and not a grain to eat," he must be thinking.

Konrad Lorenz, in his marvelously amusing and learned book about animal behavior, *King Solomon's Ring*, tells about one caged dove attacking another when Lorenz was out of the room. Lorenz didn't worry about leaving the doves alone, for, as he asks, "How could these paragons of love and virtue, these harbingers of peace, dream of harming each other?"

When he returned, however, a horrible sight met his eyes.

One dove lay on the bottom of the cage, a goodly part of him bloodly and plucked bare of feathers. Standing on top of this poor creature, "wearing the dreamy facial expression so appealing to the observer", his attacker picked mercilessly with her silver bill at her mate.

What the moral is to this tale is anybody's guess. Read into it what you will. A certain Mrs. Aesop suggests, "Pretty feathers do not necessarily a kind heart make," or "A cat may look at a king, but one dove looking at another dove's dinner is in for a terribly unpleasant surprise."

THIRTY

Canvasbacks Are Majestic.
Majestic?

Everyone is delighted when the first groups of Canvasbacks return in November. These charming ducks always arrive much later in the season than do the Canada Geese.

One often hears these ducks referred to as Redheads. However, the birds who visit Silver Lake each winter are almost always Canvasbacks. Redheads are smaller, and the males are not as white in color. The heads of Canvasbacks are much longer and leaner than those of Redheads. It is interesting to note that Canvasbacks are found only in North America, whereas a variety of Redheads, known as Pochards, is found in other parts of the world.

Like most of Delmarva's populations of ducks and geese, the Canvasbacks have nested on the great interior plains of northern Canada. But, unlike the Canadas, Canvasbacks are late migrants, preferring to linger in areas around the Great Lakes until the waters freeze and the ducks are forced by severe weather to fly south.

By mid-winter, there are usually hundreds of Canvasbacks resting on Silver Lake during the day. Winter dawn always finds the air alive with Canvasbacks returning to the lake after a night of feeding elsewhere. Airborne, they travel in family groups, whizzing through the air like small bursts of gunshot. Indeed, their swift flight has been clocked at seventy-two miles per hour! Canada Geese, when descending, float gracefully, almost lazily, toward the water. Families of Canvasbacks, in contrast, follow each other in rapid, darting succession to make their bullet-swift landings.

Canvasbacks must have a strong sense of identity, for, invariably after reaching the lake, each group swims toward a central gathering spot, with later arrivals aiming their descent so that they will hit the water near the increasingly larger and larger mass of Canvasbacks. By the time the radiance of dawn has faded into pale blue winter day, most Canvasbacks have returned to the lake, and have formed themselves into one enormous cluster of their own kind. For a short time, this tightly knit mass swims alertly but aimlessly. Then, as if on signal, almost all of them put their heads under their wings for a long day's snooze.

Winter winds blow against the sleeping little ducks, separating them. As nightfall nears, the Canvasbacks awaken. Immediately, they begin tightening their wind-scattered ranks, until once again they have become a closely packed raft numbering several hundred birds. For some hours, they engage in pre-flight manoeuvres, swimming slowly back and forth across the lake, apparently gathering all strays, and testing the wind. This they do in a seemingly impenetrable unit which other ducks and geese are careful not to invade.

Individual Canvasbacks are attractive, with their gleaming white backs and their rusty-red necks and heads; but when they move in one solid concentration across the surface of the lake, Canvasbacks attain a dynamic quality which has to be called majestic. Such an adjective may seem inappropriate applied to ducks. Nevertheless, the purposeful movement of the tightly packed mass seems like a statement of one of the immutable forces of nature --- awesome and unforgettable.

And undoubtedly is.

THIRTY-ONE

Black Clouds Overhead

The weeks before Thanksgiving should be called "The Time of the Blackbird" for it is at this season that tens of thousands of these birds gather themselves into one of their annual migratory passages over Rehoboth. On the days of their most unified flights, they rise from the trees of Rehoboth and from the marshes north of the town to form a great, spiraling, noisy stream of birds which takes half an hour or more to pass over any given location.

For weeks in advance, clouds of blackbirds drift across the fields from one small patch of woods to another, or settle in thick masses onto newly ploughed fields in search of grubs and other insects. Then, obeying some immutable natural command, all groups join together to begin the southward migration. Each year they do this, and each year they follow the same route, lifting out of Rehoboth's trees like wind-blown black smoke, to fly in thick undulating banners over the lake and south along the coast.

A flight of such incredible numbers makes itself intensely noticeable to all creatures below it. Humans stop to stare upward, and later discuss the phenomenon with wonder.

Geese on Silver Lake grow disturbed with the noise and commotion overhead and decide to take off. The racket even awakens the sleeping Canvasbacks, who pop their heads out from under their wings to see what is going on. Curious Blue Jays fly to the telephone wires for closer inspection of the event, turning and craning their heads upward in apparent amazement.

These gigantic annual sky waves of birds are usually made up of Red Wings, Blackbirds, Grackles, and Cowbirds. They have nested in the marshes in northern Delaware, in Pennsylvania, and in New Jersey. In the fall, they leave the nesting sites, gathering around farm fields in search of waste grain, until they unite for their spectacular surge to wintering grounds. A popular winter roost in Virginia's Dismal Swamp has been known to hold an estimated fifteen million birds.

Man, as is his wont, complains that these huge flocks harm the crops. As a result, bounties frequently have been placed on the birds. Some crop losses are certainly incurred. It has been shown, however, that these birds do great service to man by having as their principal diet quantities of weed seeds, as well as caterpillars, canker worms, Japanese beetles, and other insects harmful to agriculture. So before any more mass killing of Red-Wings, and other Blackbirds takes place, thus again upsetting the ecology, it might be well to remember that Blackbirds perform a beneficial service to man, and should be protected rather than destroyed.

THIRTY-TWO

Look Again, Audubon

Audubon was one of the greats, no doubt about that; marvelous painter, naturalist, conservationist, the works. But would it be possible, without raising a terrible hullabaloo, to question the fidelity of one of Audubon's bird portraits? One picture Audubon painted --- that of Blue Jays --- is the evilest portrait of a bird imaginable. Because of Audubon's enormous influence, this picture has undoubtedly prejudiced hundreds of people against Blue Jays ever since Audubon painted it.

Take a look at the picture. Three Jays are shown on a vine-entwined stump. The top Blue Jay pecks into an egg which he holds against the tree with his foot. The contents of the egg spill down into the mouth of the middle Jay. The third Jay thrusts its beak into yet another egg, from which drops of yolk are oozing. The whole scene is gruesome, leaving the impression that Blue Jays are the monsters of the bird world.

Before looking at the many delightful traits a Blue Jay has, let's examine this Blue Jay egg-eating business a minute. A definitive and much-consulted reference book, *Birds of America*, begins a lengthy article on Blue Jays like this:

"The Blue Jay . . . is one of the wickedest (of birds) . . . There can be no doubt that he is a persistent and merciless nest robber --- that he eats the eggs and kills and devours the young of smaller and defenseless birds."

There it is, in somewhat lurid prose, and okayed by the President of the Audubon Society, no less. But then, look what the end of the SAME article says:

"Stomach analysis indicates that about three-fourths of the Jay's food consists of vegetable matter and that most of this is acorns, chestnuts, beechnuts and the like. Such noxious insects as wood-boring beetles, grasshoppers, eggs of various caterpillars, and scale insects constitute about nineteen and one-half per cent of his food. Predacious beetles contribute about three and one-half per cent. This leaves but one per cent for the birds and eggs, the mice, fish, salamanders, snails, and crustaceans, that make up the remainder of his diet."

ONE PER CENT! And this tiny percentage includes not only eggs, but ALSO MICE, FISH, SALAMANDERS, SNAILS, AND CRUSTACEANS!

Apparently, even experts fall victim to a prevailing opinion, whether or not it is true, and have thus taken part in the continuance of the myth that the Blue Jay is an evil bird. Blue Jays occupy a valuable niche in the balanced system of the world. In addition, they have many positive traits.

Firstly, there can be no question that the Jay performs an invaluable service to other birds in his role as watchman and alarm-giver. Let a cat, a snake, an owl, or a hawk appear in the vicinity, and what bird is up there on the tree limb sounding the warning? The Jay, of course. His abrasive clamour may grate on YOUR ears, but on hearing the loud tocsin, all careless ground feeders immediately take cover.

It is a curious thing that most people, even many bird lovers, cling to the belief that these warning shrieks are the only sounds a Blue Jay makes. Far from it. For instance, have you ever heard two Jays talking to each other? More soft and loving chirpings were never uttered.

Years ago, we raised an abandoned baby Jay, and he grew up thinking of us as his parents. He loved to sit on a shoulder, put his head up close to an ear, (how did he know a human ear was an ear?) and then give forth with this endless love talk, all soft and confiding, and heart-melting, and obviously an expression of affection.

Or would you believe beautiful singing from a Blue Jay? You ought to, because they have a charming song; often imitative, melodious, varied, and musical. The theme and variations are not generally as prolonged as those of a Mockingbird, but they contain much of the same variety and interest.

Jays make another sound, too. If you hear a sort of noteless, rattling trill, the sound is being made by a Blue Jay. While giving this odd call, the Jay jumps rapidly up and down on a tree limb. Quite high jumps --- straight up and straight down, ten or twelve jumps at a time, and all the while issuing this rattley wooden whirrrrr. This mysterious behaviour is not confined to any particular season, but always seems to be performed when the Jay is surrounded by several other members of his family. A lesson to young jays? Territorial assertion? What?

So Blue Jays are beneficial to humans because they eat garden pests. They render invaluable service to other birds by acting as warning sirens. They sing beautifully. But wait, there is more.

Jays must be among the most courageous of living creatures. Imagine, if you will, that your own baby falls from its carriage into an inaccessible pit. While you are frantically wondering how to get the baby out, a huge monster, four hundred times your size, appears and tries to grab the baby. What would you do in this crisis? Faint, probably.

Given a similar situation, however, a Blue Jay attacks. Baby Jays do fall on the ground, with no way to get back home to the safe tree tops. Do the parent Jays give up? Never. Without thought of their own safety, they will dive bomb any intruder with such intensity that the menacing human or other predator will be forced to get under cover quickly. The Jay does more than make a feint at his enemy. He tries to break the skin, aiming always at the head and the eyes, and a sharp beak propelled by a lightning-fast Jay can cause quite a wound.

Moreover, faced with what would seem to be an almost hopeless situation, the Jays do not throw up their wings in despair. Instead, Papa and Mama continue to raise the baby Jay, making a sort of intensive-care ward out of the ground. They guide the baby bird away from dangerous open spots and into snug leaf hide-aways. They make constant trips with food. And they never leave the baby alone. Either Papa or Mama is always directly above the grounded baby. One such fallen little Jay was thus brought to handsome maturity in our back yard, despite intrusions of wandering humans, cats, and dogs. So if you find a baby bird on the ground, check carefully to see if Papa and Mama are around before adopting the orphan.

Fortunately, Blue Jays are not aware of the dim view taken of them by many people. In spite of classifications assigned by humans, in spite of Latin names, in spite of erudite or not-so-erudite articles, Blue Jays continue to flash their brilliant blue against the long cool green of pines. And, looking at them there on the pine bough, leaning toward each other in eager conversation, one feels an overwhelming sense of humility. For what Ph.D. Ornithologist knows what they are saying?

And if the great naturalist were still alive, might one say to him, "Look again, Audubon"?

IV

CODA

THIRTY-THREE

A Tick Of Time

And what will be the fate of Sussex County, and of all other places around the world not yet ruined by the march of progress --- these diminishing green gardens where the busy talk of birds still fills a summer afternoon with sweet, staccato music; where Blackeyed Susans yet can stretch long yellow scarves of brilliance across September fields; where wild geese can stop the watcher's heart with echeloned flights across a wintering sky?

Will all this soon be gone? Can our present, headlong race toward destruction of all the earth be stopped? To save any of the world will require a fundamental change in our point of view. Is this possible? Are all of us in western civilizations so steeped in the tradition of man's superiority over all other living things that our destruction of the earth is inevitable?

In the book of Genesis, considered sacred by the Christians, the Jews, and the Mohammadens, God commands Adam and Eve to "be fruitful and multiply and replenish the earth and SUBDUE IT, AND HAVE DOMINION OVER THE FISH OF THE SEA, AND OVER THE FOWL OF THE AIR, AND OVER EVERY LIVING THING THAT MOVETH UPON THE EARTH''. We have faithfully followed this command, and

187

now, with increasing technology, are continuing to do so at an ever speeded pace.

As one witnesses the results of this belief, one can only contrast it with the philosophies of primitive men who lived in harmony with the earth. Consider, for instance, the words of the great American Indian, Chief Seattle, who said, "The perfumed flowers are our sisters; the deer, the horse, the great eagle, these are our brothers. The rocky crests, the juices of the meadows, the body heat of the pony, and man --- all belong to the same family . . . . . .

"This we know. The earth does not belong to man; man belongs to the earth. All things are connected like the blood which unites one family . . . . . Even the white man, whose God walks and talks with him as friend to friend, cannot be exempt from the common destiny . . . . You may think now that you own Him . . . but you cannot. This earth is precious to Him and to harm the earth is to heap contempt on its Creator. The whites too shall pass; perhaps sooner than all other tribes. Continue to contaminate your bed, and you will one night suffocate in your own waste."

Is there room in our heritage to learn this lesson? So far, over the ages, we have not. During the Inquisition, people were burned to death because they refused to believe that the universe pivoted around the world and that the world was made exclusively for man.

You may be harboring the impression that we in the twentieth century are a long way removed from the point of view of these Inquisitors. The serenely flowing rivers of civilization have carried us through those medieval waste-

On the sign: WORLD'S END SPONSORED BY I.M.GREEDY AND C.R. POLLUTION

lands, you may think, floating our little vessels of culture onto a high island of superior knowledge and philosophy.

Would it were true.

The waters of civilized thought have remained quite still and murky over the centuries. True, individual minds have soared in musical or intellectual genius over the vast flat seas below. But few among us have really learned to walk with humility and understanding. Are there many who truly believe in the oneness of the world?

Only a handful yet know that a cat is as important as a king, and that plankton is more precious than princes. Filled with the convictions of our human superiority, we casually order the saws to slaughter trees that for two thousand years have bent their trunks to the wind. And for what? To make picnic tables?

With arrogance, we unsling the rifles and kill for fun, fun, fun, flinging the feathered or furry carcasses on our doorsteps with pride.

Eagerly, we set the traps that torture and maim. For what difference if it takes an animal days to die? Animals don't feel anything, do they? Greedily, we stun the shimmering fish with electronic devices so they may fall more easily into our nets. For fertilizer? For cat food?

Fill in that marsh! Dig up that ocean bottom! Foul that river! Gouge that hill! Spill that oil! We need trailer parks, miles of automobiles, and lots of electrical toothbrushes, don't we?

And where are they now, the white beaches, the cool wetlands, the forests, the animals, the birds, and the fish we have murdered into extinction?

This conviction of man's superiority comes to us not only from our forefathers. It is also drummed into our souls through our language itself. Look at the many phrases which use the world's creatures in a derogatory sense:

Has, for example, your catty, bird-brained sister made cow eyes at some old goat and behaved like a silly goose? Did your little shrimp of a brother come into the house dirty as a pig and eat like a hog? The beast! Did he get grumpy as a bear because he thought the food wasn't fit for a dog? Did your partner duck the issue, claw his way up, weasel out, and monkey around with a fishy deal? The worm! Let me tell you, if you don't think that's for the birds, you're cuckoo.

And tell me, pray, is there a viper or a snake in the grass

who ever dreamed up chemical warfare or hydrogen bombs? Has there ever been an animal who perpetrated a Belsen or a Dachau? When we see human mobs killing and stealing and rioting, on what basis of truth do we say that they are behaving like animals? Animals don't act like that. Like savages, maybe. Like barbarians. But not like animals.

Perhaps now is the moment to question our assumed human superiority and our doubtful right to dominate the world. Maybe, before it is too late, we should seek with a Diogenes lamp to find truth walking hand in hand with every living thing, to find glory shining from every feather, every petal, every grain of sand, to see beauty riding on the beating wing. And may we, as humans, have the grace to know that we are but specks existing for a tick of time in the wonder that is world.

THIRTY-FOUR

Thanks, But No Thanks

Most of my friends like to travel the world.
They jump into planes to be frantically hurled
To Nome or to Cairo or Timbuktu
To Jodhpur, the Congo, or Shikoku.
You name it, they've been there, they've done it all.
They've explored every tomb from Chung King to Bengal.

And when they de-plane in places exotic
They consider conventional trips idiotic.
They scorn to continue by motor or train.
Guided tours are beneath them, a bus they disdain.
Instead they choose camels to cross desert sands.
They mush behind huskies through snow-covered lands.
They teeter on mules over steep mountain tracks.
They sway atop elephants, llamas, or yaks.
They hack through deep jungles without any guides.
They search for mysterious, man-eating tribes.

All this they perform with the greatest aplomb,
As if it were not in the least venturesome.
And when they return, they bring pressure to bear
To get me to join them, by sea or by air.

"My dear, you're provincial, you simply don't know
The wonders of packing through fourteen-foot snow.
You ought to get out more. What's holding you back?

Let's travel the Yukon by sled and kayak!
How can you stay here in this backwater spot
When out there, some place else, you might find Camelot?
Come on! Pack your bags! Let's be up and away,
To Hankow by junk, to Kirenski by sleigh!
You never will know what life really is
'Til you visit Ubangi, explore old Tabriz.
Do you want to sit home all your life like a clod?
How CAN you be happier here than abroad?"

When they have finished, I say, with a sigh,
"Your words are persuasive. I cannot deny
That your trips sound terrific, exciting, fantastic.
And I don't mean to seem in the least bit sarcastic
When I ask if you think there are truths in Lahore
Which can't be learned here at my very own door.

You may say if you want that I'm like Walter Mitty
But I really don't need your compassion or pity.

Each person is different, as you very well know.
Some like to stay home, and some like to go.
There are people who yearn for the much greener grass
To be found on the far side of each mountain pass,
And others who feel there is no need to roam
When beauty is found in profusion at home.

Thoreau had a point when he said he would choose
Touring widely in Concord over any world cruise.
Don't you think it's magnificent here by the ocean?
There's much greater peace here, and far less commotion.
This County! This little oasis of green!
To me, it's as fair as the places you've seen.
A Thrush in my yard holds for me as much thrill
As any Cotinga in deepest Brazil.
I'd rather watch Sandpipers rush up this sand
Than look for Flamingos in Basutoland.
It's more comfortable here than on any train.
And it's lots less exhausting than catching a plane.

Maybe, at one time, in centuries past,
It was fun to explore all those scenes unsurpassed.
It might have been thrilling to leave from Khartoum
To find "Dr. Livingstone, here, I presume",
Or to tent on the cool snows of Kilamanjaro
With no deeper care than the hunt on the morrow,
Or to charge over sands like Arabia's Lawrence.
But now all those places are covered with torrents
Of sun-goggled tourists who spend all their days
Taking snaps with their Kodaks of peasants in drays,
And comparing the cost of palazzos in Rome
With the price of motel rooms on freeways back home.

All airports are crowded, all highways are jammed.
The places to eat and to sleep are all crammed.
I'd much rather jump from the nearest church steeple
Than to stand in long lines of impatient, cross people.

Today, to find spots that aren't tourist be-strewn
One must climb on a rocket and go to the moon.

So thanks, but no thanks, I'd rather stay here
Than fight through the crowds on this fast-shrinking sphere.
And while you are battling your way through the traffic,
I'll sit by my fire with the new Geographic
And read all about the delights of Namoxi
While I sip on a drink and travel by proxy.

So, good luck! Bon Voyage! Au Revoir! And Goodbye!
May your journey be smooth as you fly through the sky.
And while you are running for bus or for plane
Right here in this beautiful spot I'll remain,
Thanking my stars for my fortunate lot
That you're on that plane, and that I am not."